PRINTED LIGHT

PRINTED LIGHT

THE SCIENTIFIC ART OF
WILLIAM HENRY FOX TALBOT AND
DAVID OCTAVIUS HILL WITH
ROBERT ADAMSON

JOHN WARD
SCIENCE MUSEUM, LONDON

SARA STEVENSON
SCOTTISH NATIONAL PORTRAIT GALLERY, EDINBURGH

SCOTTISH NATIONAL PORTRAIT GALLERY

EDINBURGH
HER MAJESTY'S STATIONERY OFFICE

ACKNOWLEDGEMENTS   We wish to acknowledge our gratitude to our friends and colleagues for their generous assistance in the preparation of this catalogue. Particular thanks are due to Janis Adams of the National Galleries of Scotland, Douglas Arnold, David Bruce of the Scottish Film Council, Anthony Burnett-Brown, Brian Coe of the Royal Photographic Society, Claire Dart of the Science Museum, Ian Gill of the Free Church of Scotland, Miss Aileen Graham, Murray Johnston, R. E. Lassam of the Fox Talbot Museum, Julie Lawson of the Scottish Photography Archive, Alison Morrison-Low of the Royal Museum of Scotland, Ian O'Riordan of the Edinburgh City Art Centre, Larry Schaaf, Helen Smailes of the Scottish National Portrait Gallery, Robin Rodger of the Perth Museum and Art Gallery, Dr. David Thomas of the Science Museum, Susan Ward and Jane Wess of the Science Museum. We are especially grateful to Sheila Smith, Anne Jack and Jessie Hassan for the meticulous typescript.

CONTENTS

Since its invention, photography has been subject to a divisive approach: is it a FOREWORD
science? is it an art? It is symptomatic of this way of thinking that the Science
Museum in London owns the finest collection of photographs by the inventor of
the first practicable negative and positive process, Henry Fox Talbot, whilst an
art gallery, the Scottish National Portrait Gallery, owns the finest collection of
photographs using Talbot's process, by David Octavius Hill and Robert
Adamson. Talbot's photographs have been captured for the 'science' lobby and
Hill and Adamson's belong in the 'art' section.

     For the first time, in a major and significant collaboration
between the Science Museum and the Scottish National Portrait Gallery, the best
examples of the work of Talbot and the Hill-Adamson partnership have been
brought together in an exhibition and in the accompanying catalogue. The aim
has been to explore the interlocking worlds of art and science in the early
nineteenth century to see how they complemented as well as opposed each other,
and how they created a climate in which the earliest photographs proved also to
be amongst the most remarkable ever taken.

Timothy Clifford   Dr. Neil Cossons
Director   Director
National Galleries of Scotland   Science Museum

1   A CAMERA LUCIDA DRAWING, 'VILLA
    MELZI 5 OCT 1833', DESCRIBED BY
    TALBOT AS '. . . MELANCHOLY TO
    BEHOLD.'
    Science Museum, Fox Talbot Collection.

2   PORTABLE CAMERA OBSCURA USED BY
    TALBOT.
    Science Museum, Fox Talbot Collection.

3   ROSSLYN CASTLE, SKETCHING WITH A
    CAMERA OBSCURA, BY PAUL SANDBY.   Reproduced by courtesy of the Paul Mellon
                                           Collection.

WILLIAM HENRY FOX TALBOT

Early in October 1833, an English gentleman, William Henry Fox Talbot, was amusing himself sketching by the side of Lake Como in Italy. He was attempting to use a popular artist's aid of the time, a camera lucida. This instrument is essentially a prism on a supporting arm. When sited over a sheet of drawing paper it presents a reflected image which, in theory, the artist can sketch. In practice, it is fiendishly difficult to use as Talbot later recorded: 'For when the eye was removed from the prism — in which all looked beautiful — I found that the faithless pencil had only left traces on the paper melancholy to behold'[1] (Fig 1). After several fruitless attempts Talbot gave up the struggle but then thought of trying another, rather different, artist's aid he had used on previous Continental holidays, the camera obscura (Fig 2). In the portable form Talbot proposed to use, this instrument consisted of a closed box with a lens at one end. The lens projected an image via an inclined mirror, on to a glass screen. The artist could then trace the image through paper placed on the screen (Fig 3). The camera obscura is rather simpler to use than the camera lucida but it still posed problems as Talbot again noted, 'because the pressure of the hand and pencil upon the paper tends to shake and displace the instrument (insecurely fixed, in all probability, while taking a hasty sketch by a roadside, or out of an inn window); and if the instrument is once deranged, it is most difficult to get it back again, so as to point truly in its former direction. Besides which, there is another objection, namely that it baffles the skill and patience of the amateur to trace all the minute details on the paper.'[2] It was while Talbot was remembering the beauty of the image produced on the screen of the camera obscura and contemplating the labour that would be required to sketch it in all its detail that the idea occurred to him — why not coat the paper in salt of silver known to be sensitive to light and thus capture the image chemically? This simple concept was to form the basis of Talbot's invention of the negative-positive photographic process which was to earn him the title of 'Father of Modern Photography'.

Talbot was born in Melbury in Dorset in 1800, the son of Lady Elisabeth Talbot and William Davenport Talbot. He was educated at Harrow school and later Cambridge. Talbot was a gentleman, a typical member of English landed society.[3] By the standards of the day, he was not a great landowner, or exceptionally rich, but he took over the ancestral home, Lacock Abbey, in the fashionable county of Wiltshire in 1826 and lived there with his family. He briefly became a Member of Parliament for Chippenham but did not enjoy the hurly-burly of the Reform Parliament of 1832 and soon gave up his seat. It was in 1832 that he married Constance Mundy, who bore him three daughters and a son. Like many gentlemen of the period he had a London retreat, rooms in Sackville Street, Piccadilly, to which he retired when he was not required to be at home or take part in the summer social round of visiting friends and relations in the great country houses of England. Talbot, of course, had no specific occupation apart from managing the estate but, again like many gentlemen, he was interested in scholarship. He made a special study of Assyriology and etymology but his deepest interest, by far, was science.

From his earliest days to his death Talbot was interested in nature and natural phenomena but his interest in science proper began at Harrow school where he was fortunate enough to be able to study physics and chemistry outside the curriculum. This stood him in good stead when he went up to university. At Cambridge, Talbot took the Mathematical Tripos course at a time when according to one authority, it was becoming 'a highly specialised training in mathematics and theoretical physics unique in its scientific context, its specialism and its steady historical development'. The final examination is adjudged to have been 'the highest intellectual hurdle in the country and those who acquitted themselves well in it were men of mark'.[4] Talbot acquitted himself very well indeed although he did not come first in the year, which his family and many of his friends confidently expected. What can be said is that at a time when scientific education in England in general compared unfavourably with scientific education in Scotland and on the continent of Europe, Talbot probably had the best the country could offer.

Talbot's scientific interests were wide ranging. As well as having a sound knowledge of physics and chemistry, he was a formidable mathematician and had a life-long love of botany and horticulture. He published well over fifty scientific papers and took out twelve English patents.[5] He became a Fellow of the Royal Astronomical Society at the age of twenty-two and a Fellow of the Royal Society when he was only thirty-one. Talbot's inherent gifts of a keen intellect and analytical mind coupled with a deep understanding of mathematics and an innate curiosity about the natural world made him particularly suited to science.

At this point it is pertinent to note that although Talbot will be described as 'a scientist', the term was coined in his lifetime. It was only during the 19th century that organised science began to be practised in England in the form we understand it today. After a century of almost awe-atruck acceptance, the works of Isaac Newton were beginning to be questioned and re-evaluated. Talbot's attitudes were therefore influenced by conflicting philosophies and it is not surprising that he should sometimes seem to be of two different worlds. He took a keen interest in the new ideas and the popular scientific preoccupations of the day, but occasionally his views looked back to the 18th century and his attitude to nature was at times almost Romantic.

It might be argued that it took a man with the dual cultural background of Talbot to invent photography. An 18th-century philosopher, Locke, is reputed to have sat inside a camera obscura and pondered on the nature of reality as he observed the ephemeral images on the wall before him.[6] It was perhaps the 18th-century part of Talbot's mind which, when remembering his use of a portable form of the same instrument, led him to 'reflect on the inimitable beauty of the pictures of nature's paintings which the glass lens of the camera throws upon the paper in its focus — fairy pictures, creations of a moment and destined as rapidly to fade away'. But it was surely a 19th-century mind, trained in optics and chemistry and with a belief in systematic experiment which prompted the reasoning that followed:

'How charming it would be if it were possible to cause those natural images to imprint themselves durably on the paper!

And why should it not be possible? I asked myself . . . Now Light, where it exists, can exert an action, and, in certain circumstances does exert one sufficient to cause changes in material bodies. Suppose, then, such an action could be executed on the paper; and suppose the paper could be visibly changed by it. In that case surely some effect must result having a general resemblance to the cause which produced it: so that the variegated scene of light and shade might leave its image or impression behind . . .

And since according to chemical writers, the nitrate of silver is a substance peculiarly sensitive to the action of light, I resolved to make a trial of it'.[7]

Accounts of the trials and their consequences were given in a variety of sources, notably *The Pencil of Nature* and a paper Talbot presented to the Royal Society on 31 January 1839.[8] After repeated experiments Talbot found that a series of coatings of weak silver chloride solutions on paper were the most promising and in the spring of 1834 he was able to obtain 'distinct and

4 TALBOT'S SOLAR MICROSCOPE.
Science Museum, Fox Talbot Collection.

Latticed Window
(with the Camera Obscura)
August 1835

*When first made, the squares
of glass about 200 in number
could be counted, with help
of a lens.*

5 THE EARLIEST SURVIVING CAMERA
NEGATIVE, WITH COMMENTS IN
TALBOT'S HAND.
Science Museum, Fox Talbot Collection.

6 FIRST SMALL CAMERAS USED BY
TALBOT, c.1835-1839.
Science Museum, Fox Talbot Collection.

pleasing images of such things as leaves, lace, and other flat objects of complicated forms and outlines by exposing them to the light of the sun.'[9] These were of course, direct contact copies: no camera was involved. Indeed, when he tried his paper in the camera obscura Talbot found the image formed far too faint to be acceptable. It was only after further experiments that he was able to produce a more sensitive paper. The first pictures Talbot made using an optical system were, in fact, made by projecting the light of the sun down the tube of a microscope (Fig 4). To continue using Talbot's own words, it was only 'when I had succeeded in fixing the images of the solar microscope by means of a peculiarly sensitive paper, there appeared no longer any doubt that an analogous process would succeed in copying the objects of external nature'.[10] The earliest surviving camera negative made by Talbot dates from the summer of 1835. The pictures made at this time were very small and only appeared after an exposure of at least half an hour in the camera (Fig 5).

Having reached this point, Talbot found other matters to occupy his mind and on his own admission three years passed during which time very little was added to his previous knowledge. Talbot was to regret his lack of urgency for early in 1839 news came of a French process which seemed to be identical to his own. The process discovered by Louis Jacques Mandé Daguerre was, in fact very different to Talbot's. The images, called daguerreotypes, were indeed made in a camera obscura but were direct positives produced on copper plates thinly coated with silver which had been made light sensitive by iodine vapour. Talbot was not to know this at the time and hastened to publish details of his own work. His art was clearly in a primitive state and the camera pictures were still very small. Talbot's process, however, had one advantage over Daguerre's which was to be of critical importance. Hidden away in Talbot's Royal Society paper, under a section dealing with the copying of engravings, it was noted that although the lines of the original were faithfully copied, the lights and shadows were reversed. The paper went on: 'If the picture so obtained is *first preserved* so as to bear sunshine, it may be afterwards employed as an object to be copied; and by means of this second process the lights and shadows are brought back to their original disposition'.[11] Talbot had first practised this technique early in 1835 but it is possible that even he did not fully appreciate the significance of his discovery. The evidence suggests that almost all the images Talbot showed in those early months of 1839 were negatives. It is clear from all the contemporary records that Talbot, and others who attempted his process did not find it easy to produce positive prints. Yet Talbot had discovered the principle which was to make his process the basis of modern photography — the negative which could be used to make an unlimited number of positive prints.

The announcement of the two processes, almost simultaneously, aroused tremendous interest and speculation. Few of the early commentators could have actually seen a photograph, which was not surprising as there were not many to see, but this did not blunt their enthusiasm. Some, like Talbot before them, assumed that the two processes were the same and inevitably in such a situation there was muddle and confusion in the minds of reporters and public. *The Mechanics Magazine* for February published an account of a method 'invented by a M. Daguerre of Paris' but concluded its article by citing the examples shown at the Royal Institution of London. These were not daguerreotypes but Talbot's Photogenic Drawings shown when Michael Faraday announced the process on 25 January 1840. The article included the wonderful phrase, 'by some the discovery of this use of sunshine was thought to be moonshine, but we are happy to say that it appears likely to be turned to some practical purpose'.[12] On 20 April *The Magazine of Science* recorded, almost with dismay, that 'we have taken no notice of the extraordinary process of Photogenic Drawing which now occupies such general attention'.[13] On the same day another weekly journal *The Mirror* filled its front page with what it called a 'Facsimile of a Photogenic Drawing'[14] (Fig 8). In its next issue it noted that this facsimile had 'produced a much greater sensation that we had anticipated'.[15] Similar facsimiles were published in *The Magazine of Science* where they were evidently equally well received.[16] These facsimiles are the first published pictures produced by the printing press from photographically derived images. Again in *The Mechanics Magazine* of 30 March, a Mr. Cumberland, writing from Bristol, reported: 'The liberal disclosures of Mr. Talbot have set many people to work here in copying lace, prints and leaves, by means of the direct rays of the sun'.[17] Talbot's friends were no less enthusiastic about his process. Lady Theresa Digby wrote to him from Windsor on 13 April: 'Many thanks for the drawings which I showed to the Queen yesterday after dinner. They met with universal admiration from a large party'.[18] At the end of May, Talbot's old Housemaster from Harrow wrote to him in equally flattering terms: 'My Dear Talbot You are an arrant cheat or, at best an aider and abetter in deception. Before opening your packet of Photogenic drawings, I was so completely taken in by your lace-picture that like a dutiful husband, I was actually handing it over to Mrs. Butler as a lace pattern — intended for her, — before I discovered my mistake. And then the leaves!'[19]

All this enthusiasm, however, soon became tinged with caution and then dismay as would-be photographers tried the art themselves and experienced its problems. Talbot's cousin wrote to him at the end of March that a representation of an etching that at first was beautiful had since faded away. He went on: 'Everybody here is mad for photogeny but I have not yet burnt my fingers with it intending first to see it performed by a professor'.[20] It was a great source of irritation that neither Talbot nor Daguerre had published explicit operational details of their respective processes and it is clear that what had been published had been imperfectly understood. *The Mechanics Magazine* of 23 March had noted that some photogenic drawings sent to them by a Mr. Hemming and those of Talbot were not 'worth for a moment the attention of the artist, for, besides other defects the lights and shades are reversed'.[21] *The Mirror* confirmed that the nature of Talbot's negative-positive technique had not been grasped by recording the surprise of a Mr. Havell who 'having attempted to copy Rembrandt's powerful etching of an old man reading found that the photographic proof made a most ludicrous metamorphosis for, instead of a white man with black hair, it exhibited a black man with white hair and white eyes'.[22] Even when people had access to the best information that was available they still experienced problems. In Scotland, Andrew Fyfe, Vice-President of the Society of Arts, found the results very uncertain. He recorded: 'In preparing paper by this method, it is very difficult to get the chloride uniformally spread over its surface, and accordingly when exposed to light, it often gives a variety of shades; indeed in many places it continues white'. He also found it difficult to fix his photographs using Talbot's recommendations, potassium iodide or common salt. Of the latter he noted: 'I have repeatedly failed in preserving specimens in this way'.[23] There can be little doubt that at this time satisfactory images could only be produced with difficulty and not at all consistently, especially those made with the camera. Many of the early enthusiasts soon became discouraged and abandoned the art. The position was summed up by Robert Hunt some two years later:

'The photographic processes appeared, when first reported, to be so simple, that most persons conceived they could procure, without trouble, specimens

7   PHOTOGENIC DRAWING, A PLANT
    IMPRESSION, c.1839.
    Science Museum, Fox Talbot Collection.

The Mirror
OF
LITERATURE, AMUSEMENT, AND INSTRUCTION.

No. 945.]   SATURDAY, APRIL 20, 1839.   [PRICE 2d.

FAC-SIMILE OF A PHOTOGENIC DRAWING.

VOL. XXXIII.   R

8   THE FIRST PRINTED REPRODUCTION OF
    A PHOTOGRAPH. FACSIMILE OF A
    PHOTOGENIC DRAWING FROM THE
    MIRROR 20 APRIL 1839.
    Science Museum.

of equal beauty with those exhibited by the artist and the philosopher . . . It requires but the slightest consideration to convince us, that an element inappreciably subtile, must, in its action on chemical preparations, be affected by the most trifling change; and that differences beyond detection by any other test, would become glaringly evident under the influence of light.

Failure damped the ardour of the pursuit, and owing to the uncertainty of the results with the sensitive paper, and the delicacy of the manipulation required for the silver plate, coupled with its most unfortunate expense, the enthusiasts of the moment wearied, and at length resigned the task they had felt so certain of accomplishing, displeased that they had met with difficulties, where none were anticipated.'

Hunt went on to say: 'Photography does not possess the advantages of perfection, any more than other Human inventions. Had it been left where we found it when the discovery was announced, it would have remained a beautiful, but almost useless thing — a philosophic toy, which lent a little assistance to the cultivation of taste, but afforded none to the economy of manufactures'.[24] That photography did not remain a 'useless thing' was largely due to the persistence and imagination of Talbot.

In 1839 Talbot was in no doubt as to the primitive state of his process or that in several important respects it compared unfavourably with the rival French process. On 9 May Herschel wrote to Talbot from Paris describing the daguerreotypes he had seen: 'It is hardly saying too much to call them miraculous. Certainly they surpass anything I could have conceived as within the bounds of reasonable expectation.'[25] Up until the beginning of 1839 Talbot had worked on photography intermittently and without urgency. But now, as his notebook shows, he plunged into a period of concentrated work to improve his process.[26] In February he carried out a series of comparative tests on fixing agents and found that 'Hyposulphite of soda' and strong solutions of common salt were the most promising. In April Talbot experimented with a substance that was to be significant in the future, gallic acid, and found that it increased the 'sensibility' of bromide paper. In May and June it is clear that he was working on a variety of means of preparing sensitive papers. At the same time the notebook shows that he evolved a variety of practices which refined his techniques. He was particularly concerned to determine the most suitable paper for his work; he mentions experiments to remove watermarks, and the idea of waxing the paper negatives to make them transparent is recorded. The apparatus was not neglected; the concept of fitting additional lenses of shorter focus for copying near objects is noted and there is also a mention of 'telescope pictures'. Throughout all this period and on into 1840 he was also experimenting with copper plates and the rival daguerreotype process. At this time the French process could produce a larger and more detailed camera picture than anything Talbot could make on paper. It may be that he was experimenting with daguerreotypes to see if he could use elements of the process to improve his own. Curiously, although Talbot must have made scores of them, not a single example seems to have survived. Yet, despite all this effort, it seems likely that Talbot was still enjoying only limited success in his attempts to produce camera pictures. Of the ninety-three photogenic drawings he exhibited at the Birmingham meeting of the British Association in August 1839, a body he would certainly have been keen to impress, only twenty-one were camera pictures and all were views of Lacock Abbey.[27] A month or so later his mother wrote to him: 'I wish very much you would choose the very best Camera Obscura that is to be had, and let me give you. I am sure your discovery would be perfect . . . if you had a better instrument to work with, & it is worth anything to your celebrity to possess such a one.'[28]

Talbot's photographic experiments continued through the winter of 1839 and by the spring of 1840 his work began to bear fruit. He had made no single significant advance but a series of small improvements enabled him to produce photographs of considerably better quality. In May 1840 *The Literary Gazette* reported: 'We have been gratified by an examination of a series of photogenic drawings which Mr. Talbot has produced during his spring residence in the country; and certainly they are not only beautiful in themselves but highly interesting in regard to art. The representation of objects is perfect.'[29] It is clear also that Talbot had widened the range of his subjects. As well as the camera views of Lacock that Talbot had shown in 1839, he was now able to produce views 'of Bowood; of trees; of old walls and buildings, with implements of husbandry; of carriages; of tables covered with breakfast things; of busts and statues; and, in short, of every matter from a botanical specimen to a fine landscape, from an ancient record, to an ancient abbey'.[30] Many of the negatives from this period feature the tools and implements, wheels and ladders, which some modern writers have claimed to see as having a symbolic significance and as key elements in Talbot's work. An alternative explanation is that they were simply the everyday artefacts that happened to be lying about the grounds of Lacock Abbey. The variety of shapes and surfaces they presented made them interesting subjects for Talbot's camera, especially when tastefully arranged in groups, but the essential characteristic was that they were all static and could be captured by the, still, long exposures.

Talbot had made progress but, perhaps discouraged because in most respects his process was still inferior to the daguerreotype, his photographic work slackened during the summer. As autumn approached he confessed to Herschel that his attention to photography had been 'desultory and divided' and that the art remained 'in status quo'.[31] Yet within a few days Talbot recommenced experiments with gallic acid. He mixed it with silver nitrate and acetic acid to make what he called 'an exciting liquid'.[32] On 23 September he used this to sensitise photogenic drawing paper. He found that when he exposed this paper only briefly in the camera an invisible or latent image was produced which could be made visible by further application of the gallic acid solution. The consequences were dramatic. Exposure times were reduced to a few minutes. The range and scope of Talbot's art was immeasurably broadened. Most importantly, he could now take portraits and other living subjects. Talbot named his new process 'Calotype' from the Greek, *kalos,* meaning beautiful.

Although Talbot proposed to patent the calotype process, an exercise that was later to cause him much pain, he always intended that it should be freely practised by amateurs and, particularly, scientists. His announcement of the process early in 1841 stimulated a new wave of interest in photography. In England, calotype photography was practised almost exclusively by amateurs but the patent had not been extended to Scotland which was to have interesting consequences. This was a period for photography when, if the essential elements of the art had now been established, careful manipulation was required if failure was to be avoided. The process was still capable of enough improvement for each exercise to be a voyage of discovery and for each calotypist to feel he was a pioneer. It was an exciting period to be a photographer. Something of the magic and an indication of the effort required to produce photographs during the early 1840s is conveyed in an account written by Robert Graham, some thirty years later:

'In beautiful summer weather, operations began. But how shall we describe the anxiety with which the first results were looked for, and the disappointment which fell on all hearts and faces, when the blurred and hazy outline of an old lady, who had sat for twenty minutes in full sun-light appeared? We had expected great things, and such a result was hard to bear. But it became manifest after a few attempts that we were nevertheless at the peristyle of that temple which none of us doubted would in time be filled with gems which no artist, however exquisite, could rival . . . in those days it was expedient to divest yourself of your coat and invest yourself in a blouse or old greatcoat, to save your garments from the greenish-black stains and smudgings they were sure otherwise to receive. All available tubs, buckets, footpails, wash-hand basins and every sort of vessel which would contain water, were laid hold for the frequent washings and soakings which were required. Every room which could be darkened was needed for drying in the dark. The region of every domestic in a household was invaded, and servants were kept running perpetually with pails of hot and cold water, warm smoothing irons, etc. The whole establishment was turned topsy-turvy while its superiors were bent on photographic studies . . . for it was a most fascinating study, because coarse and brown and poor though those pictures produced were, when compared with those now obtained by the improved process, the operator was irresistibly drawn onward by the conviction that experience and care would lead to more satifactory results. Generally, each picture was an improvement on its predecessor because the time of exposure in the camera, the proper amount of development, and the due strength of the solutions were being ascertained. The art manifestly had great capabilities, and the operator was pleased with the hope of being able to succeed in bringing them out.'[33]

From the announcement of the calotype process in 1841 to the end of 1843, Talbot took a great proportion of the photographs for which he is best known today. He made calotype views of architectural subjects in several parts of England and in 1843 made a successful photographic expedition to France. Portraits and groups featuring his family, servants and friends were also produced in large numbers and he took a number of interesting studies of working men. For a period Talbot seems to have enjoyed simulating scenes, such as a group selling fruit and flowers, or action shots such as sawing wood. All these groups would have been carefully posed of course, but some of them manage to look surprisingly spontaneous. Amongst the most natural and charming portraits are those of his family, particularly his young daughters, and these would not look out of place in a snapshot album of some fifty years later. Talbot also continued to produce scores of calotypes of trees, plants, flowers, leaves, still life studies, sculpture, statuary, and copies of engravings, etchings, paintings, books, maps, letters, music and the like.

It is clear that Talbot felt that a great deal of work still remained to be done to refine his process. The notebooks show that, at least until April 1843,[34] he continued his experiments on several different aspects of photography, some of the fruits of his labours resulting in the photographic patent of June 1843.[35] It was about this time that Talbot finally decided to make exclusive use of the fixing agent used by photographers today, hyposulphite. Although Talbot had first used hyposulphite at Herschel's suggestion in 1839, since his comparative tests of that year he had generally favoured common salt or sometimes potassium bromide or potassium iodide. Talbot had found salt a satifactory fixer, but others, whilst appreciating the beauty of the results when successful, experienced problems. Talbot's cousin, Christopher Rice Mansell Talbot, wrote to him in August 1842: 'I am not at all satisfied with the method of fixing which you use for I find the calotypes fade very fast'.[36] In March 1843,

9   TOOLS AND WHEEL, A PHOTOGENIC
    DRAWING BY TALBOT, PROBABLY 1840.
    Science Museum, Fox Talbot Collection.

10 HORATIA FEILDING, TALBOT'S
    HALF-SISTER, ON A SOFA. A CALOTYPE,
    '20 APRIL 1842'.
    Science Museum, Fox Talbot Collection.

W. Holland Furlong of Dublin was also writing to complain of fixing difficulties: 'Sir, Though personally unknown to you, I take the liberty of addressing a few lines to you on the calotype. Sir David Brewster some months ago sent you a negative picture which I made in the County of Wicklow and which you were kind enough to positive for me. I have never been able to preserve the positives without making them a disagreeable red colour, very unlike the beautiful lilac of your positive pictures. Will you be kind enough to let me know how you prepare and preserve your chloride pictures'.[37] Although Talbot had published instructions on the calotype process, it is evident that it was always liable to failure and very careful manipulations were required. Many experimenters published their own pet modified versions of Talbot's process but there is no evidence to suggest that they gave any more consistent results. Not for the first time Talbot was criticised for excessive secrecy. George Cundell later claimed: 'Had Mr. Talbot thought fit to publish directions for the detail and refinement of his process, as minute and explicit as those given by M. Daguerre, this invention, it is probable, would now have stood in a very different position.'[38] However, a sympathetic contemporary is reported as suggesting that where Talbot went wrong was 'when writing his description of his calotype process [he] assumed his readers had brains.'[39]

Talbot himself was getting good results and sent gifts of calotypes to all his family and friends. His aunt, Lady Mary Cole, managing to curb her enthusiasm, wrote to him in October 1841: 'I am quite pleased with your very handsome present of Calotypes, they have amused and interested me very much as well as my friends. There is one, such an admirable likeness of Sir Charles Lemon that it gave me a sensation & I wish I had all my equally loved friends in the same style'.[40] Talbot's uncle, the diplomat, William Fox Strangways, was a little more generous: 'My Dear Henry, Since I have received your beautiful calotypes, such a packet as that I can always have through F.O. [Foreign Office]. I particularly admired the Hayrick. The Breakfast table & folds of the table cloth prove to me that it would be invaluable to a painter for taking off natural copies of a difficult & troublesome part of the art, namely draperies in which many good artists fail. I wish some fine day you would take the Cathedrals of Salisbury or the Abbey of Bath, & would the Avon at Clifton do as well as the Thames at Wapping?'[41] Talbot's scientific friend Herschel was positively bursting with enthusiasm a few months later: 'My Dear Sir, A great many thanks to you for the exquisite specimens of the Calotype which surpass anything I had heard of. The power of depicting scenes of conversation and acting between living persons is a wonderful stride'.[42]

Talbot had hopes that professional portraits made by the calotype process would be as successful as those made in the daguerreotype studios which were becoming more and more popular. In August 1841 he licensed the first professional calotypist, a miniature painter, Henry Collen. Collen's calotype portraits were at first well received and certain advantages over the rival daguerreotype process were recognised as the following account demonstrates:

'We have been favoured by Mr. Collen, of Somerset Street, Portman Square, with a sight of his extensive collection of photographic portraits, taken by the calotype process. Nothing can be more admirable than the extreme accuracy of the likenesses: they are free from the defect which constitutes the common objection to this kind of portraiture, namely, the ghastly corpse-like hue given to the complexion. The operation is simple, and of very short duration: a sitting of a few seconds is all that is required for taking a portrait of which any number of copies may be produced. Among the likenesses exhibited to us were those of the French Ambassador, Mr. Young the performer, Landseer the

11 TAKING A CALOTYPE PORTRAIT, c.1842.
Science Museum, Fox Talbot Collection.

12 ROBERT HUNT, PIONEER
PHOTOGRAPHER AND AUTHOR OF THE
FIRST SUBSTANTIAL PHOTOGRAPHIC
INSTRUCTION BOOK. CALOTYPE BY
HILL AND ADAMSON.
Reproduced by courtesy of the Glasgow School
of Art.

13 GROUP AT LACOCK ABBEY, A CALOTYPE,
c.1843.
Science Museum, Fox Talbot Collection.

painter, Professor Henslow, and many distinguished persons. Mr. Collen is the only person licensed by the patentee to take portraits by this process.'[43] Unfortunately for Talbot the project did not live up to expectations. Collen experienced the usual technical difficulties and made the familiar complaint that essential details of technique were withheld from him. That neither he nor Talbot showed any particular flair for business was also a handicap. The project finally foundered but not before it had brought a certain amount of welcome publicity to the calotype. Talbot had circulated examples of his work amongst his family and friends, but although a little was being written few actual calotypes were being seen by the wider public. It may have been a realisation of this which prompted Talbot to think of publishing a book of his calotypes. Talbot could have produced a book made up of pretty photographs and there is some evidence to suggest that this is what he originally had in mind. It is to his credit that some time in 1843 Talbot chose not to do this but instead decided that he would show 'a collection of genuine specimens of the art, in most of its branches.'[44] Early in 1844 Talbot set up a printing establishment at Reading with his one time valet and now assistant, Nicholaas Henneman, in charge. It was at the Reading printing establishment that the calotypes used in the world's first commercial photographically illustrated book, *The Pencil of Nature*, were made. Talbot's publication was issued in six parts between June 1844 and April 1846. When completed it contained twenty-four calotypes and an accompanying text which outlined Talbot's conception and invention of photography and some accompanying notes of rather uneven value and quality. The most revealing aspect of the venture was Talbot's choice of images which was a statement of what he thought was important in photography. The greatest number were views of buildings, architecture, or street scenes; there were several still life studies and a number of copies; there was only one view depicting living persons and one that might be interpreted as an attempt at photographic art.

The publication of the first parts of *The Pencil of Nature* in 1844 was a landmark in Talbot's career for it marks the beginning of the end of the period which saw the invention of his photographic process. From this time on Talbot's photographic interests were to be diverted into other channels. *The Pencil of Nature* represents a fractionally small proportion of Talbot's total output of calotypes but it contains all the essential elements and is a statement of his utilitarian view of photography. This is not to say that all his images are coldly functional. As Lady Eastlake was to later note in her inimitable flowery style, 'no photographic picture that ever was taken, in heaven, or earth, or in the waters underneath the earth, of any thing, or scene, however defective when measured by an artistic scale, is destitute of a special, and what we may call an historic interest. Every form which is traced by light is the impress of one moment, or one hour, or one age in the great passage of time.'[45] The calotypes Talbot produced were made by a practical man yet, inevitably, they reflect the man and the society in which he lived.

14 TITLE PAGE, *THE PENCIL OF NATURE,* 1844.
Science Museum, Fox Talbot Collection.

TALBOT'S APPROACH TO THE CALOTYPE

Talbot felt compelled to issue slips in some early issues of *The Pencil of Nature* with a note emphasising that the photographs were 'impressed by the agency of Light alone.' A common feature in almost all of the contemporary reviews of the photographs was the sense of wonder that all this could be achieved by light and the way light and shade were depicted by the calotype. *The Art Union* noted that these 'sun pictures' were 'a transfer to paper of the masses and tracery of light and shade by means utterly inimitable by the ordinary resources of art'.[46] Central to the understanding of all Talbot's photographs is his feeling for light. Talbot was fascinated by light. Of the forty-two purely scientific papers he published at least thirty-two deal with aspects of light or optics. The invention of photography itself is a manifestation of his interest. It should be stressed that Talbot's attitude did not arise in a vacuum for it was a reflection of one of the more persistent undercurrents of contemporary science and culture in England.

The English preoccupation with light can be traced back to the publication of Newton's *Opticks* at the beginning of the 18th century.[47] Newton was a giant of the age, immensely influential far beyond the field of science. When Pope wrote 'God said, "Let Newton be!" and all was light',[48] it was a statement with several layers of truth. That light should be made up of a spectrum of colours was a fact to promote wonder and because it was the source of colour, for the rich crop of 18th-century poets it became synonymous with beauty. Later in the century the Romantic poets became more sceptical of the 'cold Philosophy' which in Keats's words sought to 'Unweave a rainbow'.[49] By the early 19th century scientists were beginning to question some of Newton's concepts but the feeling that light had a special, almost mystical, quality persisted. One of the most influential writers of the period, William Paley, recorded with approval a friend's statement that 'if light had been made by a common artist, it would have been of one uniform colour'.[50] A few years earlier the young Humphry Davy is reputed to have written: 'What we mean by nature is a series of images: but these are constituted by light. Hence the worshipper of Nature is a worshipper of light'.[51] This was surely true of the Talbot who could write 'What is Nature, but one great field of wonders past our comprehension'.[52] His delight in the play of light on different surfaces and textures and the way it is recorded by the camera was shown in Plates III and IV of *The Pencil of Nature*. The 'unlimited variety' of effects made possible by altering the direction of light is discussed specifically in his views of the bust *Patroclus* but is evident in so many of his other photographs. Talbot had a fine eye for line and mass and form which grew out of his preoccupation and he must have taken a special pleasure in those views taken over water with all the complex possibilities opened up by reflections. It is, however, important to note that the practical part of Talbot also saw a utilitarian function for the calotypes mentioned above. The photographs of china and glass were seen as a convenient way of making an accurate record, '. . . and should a thief afterwards purloin the treasures — if the mute testimony of the picture were to be produced in court — it would certainly be evidence of a rare kind.'[53] The views of busts and statuary like *Patroclus* were seen as an invaluable source of information and instruction for the artist; they also served as very convenient static test subjects for Talbot's camera.

Talbot always placed great emphasis on the accuracy with which copies of paintings, etchings and engravings could be produced and obviously felt that one of the most valuable characteristics of his art was that such copies could be easily duplicated in large numbers. Robert Hunt also recognised the value of Talbot's process in this respect and considered that this was one area

15   W. H. F. TALBOT BY JOHN MOFFAT, 1864.
Science Museum, Fox Talbot Collection.

where the daguerreotype process was definitely inferior: 'The multiplication of pictures from an original photograph is the great end of the art. The attempts made to engrave the Daguerreotype plate are all of them, to a certain extent, failures, the finer details being lost, and the "aerial perspective" entirely destroyed. Indeed, the employment of strong nitric acid, to etch the tracery marked out by the finger of light, appears as much as if it were to employ a smith to rivet the downy feather to the wing of a butterfly.'[54] The reason for this interest in reproducing images in large numbers must again be considered in a wider context. The process of industrialisation and mechanisation which accelerated in Britain during the second half of the 18th century and continued throughout Talbot's lifetime in the 19th century, had a profound effect on contemporary thought. Thomas Carlyle summed up a widespread attitude when he wrote: 'No individual now hopes to accomplish the poorest enterprise single handed and without mechanical aids . . . Philosophy, Science, Art, Literature, all depend on machinery.'[55]

The application of technology to the reproduction and multiplication of illustrations became one of the preoccupations of the age. During the early years of the 19th century there was an extraordinary interest in mechanical and optical aids to drawing (two of the most popular being the camera lucida and the camera obscura). As the century progressed, technology became more and more involved with art and design. By 1848 W. Cooke Taylor in *The Art Union* could pronounce: 'Now a great but silent revolution has been taking place in the production of works of Art for more than a century. The whole tendency of modern invention is to facilitate the multiplication of copies, and to perfect accuracy in copying.'[56] All this activity was, in part, a product of innovation in the printing industry, which had been revitalised by the effects of the Industrial Revolution after 300 years of technological stagnation. Lithography was introduced to England early in the 19th century and electrotyping invented in 1839. But it was much more than just a simple reflex response to a new technology for there was also a deep and increasing public interest in British art and design which found full expression in the Great Exhibition of 1851. It is against this background that Talbot's persistent promotion of his process as a means of duplicating works of art must be assessed, for he could copy any painting or drawing with fidelity of line. He could also make perfectly proportioned copies larger or smaller as desired.

Talbot knew that there was a potential market waiting to be exploited. It is not clear how many were produced or sold but copies of paintings, engravings, and prints feature prominently on surviving lists of Talbot's calotypes. In *The Pencil of Nature,* he felt it worth while to mention this application of his art on two separate occasions. With Plate XI he noted: 'All kinds of engravings may be copied by photographic means: this application of the art is a very important one'. And again with Plate XXIII he recorded: 'This plate is intended to show another important application of the photographic art. Facsimiles can be made from original sketches of the old masters, and thus they may be preserved from loss, and multiplied to any extent'.

As well as seeing photography as a convenient system for copying and multiplying works of art, Talbot saw it as a means of recording subjects of scenes which the artist might use as a model or, in the right hands, an artistic medium in its own right. It was certainly a different medium for, as he noted, 'it will enable us to introduce into our pictures a multitude of details which add to the truth and reality of representation, but whuch no artist would take the trouble to copy faithfully from nature.' It could also be used in the conventional artistic way as he noted, 'to awaken a train of thoughts and feelings, and picturesque imaginings.'[57] Yet it is doubtful if Talbot was especially interested in photography as art, or saw himself as an artist. He was certainly not encouraged to believe he had any artistic taste by his family. Thomas Malone reported the occasion when Talbot was taking the photograph later to become 'The Ladder', Plate XIV of *The Pencil of Nature*. Henry Collen, a respected painter of miniatures, was present and questioned Talbot's camera position: 'You are not going to take it that way surely!'. When Talbot replied that he could not take it any other way, Collen is reputed to have exclaimed: 'As an artist, I would not take it at all.'[58] It has been suggested that the story is apocryphal, but that it was repeated and published must say something about Talbot's reputation as an artist. The calotypes in *The Pencil of Nature* were considered as works of art by many contemporary reviewers and, generally, were received favourably. But later, when other calotypists began to show their work, Talbot was put firmly in his place. According to Robert Hunt in *The Art Union*, 'Many of the productions by the patentee of the Calotype process — Mr. Fox Talbot — involving the use of the gallonitrate of silver, may be seen at his place of business in Regent Street: they are extremely beautiful, but inferior, on the whole, to the artistic photography of Messrs. Hill and Adamson of Edinburgh, or those of several members of the Photographic Club.'[59] This view may not be completely objective as Hunt was a member of the recently formed Photographic Club, which was already finding Talbot's patent irksome, and he was later to be actively hostile.

'The Open Door', Plate VI of *The Pencil of Nature*, is often cited as the classic example of Talbot's artistic photography. In fact, this is an early work, probably dating from 1840 or 1841. It is one of a small group of similar photographs of a style which Talbot seems to have rarely practised again. There are one or two of his later calotypes where he was obviously imitating paintings but these are not his best or his most characteristic works. It has been suggested that Talbot had a deep and profound involvement with art, the time he spent sketching and his interest in Italian art in the 1820s being put forward as evidence. However, most young gentlemen of the period were taught to draw, particularly if they were interested in botany, and a few youthful Italian swallows do not make an artistic summer. The text in *The Pencil of Nature* shows he was acqainted with the Dutch school of art but that would not be surprising for he was an educated and cultured man and it was a style that had long been popular in England. Although Talbot was often urged by his family to seek co-operation from an artist, he seems to have found it easy to ignore these suggestions. The exception was the daguerreotypist, Antoine Claudet. Claudet was also an eminent man of science in his own right and Talbot clearly found his company congenial. All the evidence suggests that Talbot was diffident about the use of his invention as a creative artistic medium. His attitude is revealed in his 'Introductory Remarks' to *The Pencil of Nature:* '... and though we may not be able to conjecture with any certainty what rank they may hereafter attain to as pictorial productions, they will surely find their own sphere of utility, both for completeness of detail and correctness of perspective.' His real interest is revealed in a letter he wrote to Herschel in March 1841: 'I have taken a patent for the calotype, but nevertheless intend that the use of it shall be entirely free to the scientific world . . . There appears to me to be no end to the prospect of scientific research which photography has opened out.'[60]

If there is one single over-riding objective in Talbot's photographs, it is to record information. This concern can be seen in all his writings and is supported by vast numbers of his calotypes. For Talbot, it was a source of wonder that photography could record so accurately and with such detail. In his first plate of *The Pencil of Nature,* 'Part of Queen's College, Oxford', he is using the camera to present information and draw conclusions: 'This building presents on its surface the most evident marks of the injuries of time and weather, in the abraded state of the stone, which probably was of bad quality originally.'[61] The theme comes through again in Plate III, 'Articles of China', where Talbot notes: 'The more strange and fantastic the forms of his old teapots, the more advantage in having their pictures given instead of their descriptions.' And again in another view of Queen's College, Plate XIII: 'Sometimes inscriptions and dates are found upon the buildings or printed placards most irrelevant, are discovered upon their walls; sometimes a distant dialplate is seen, and upon it — unconsciously recorded — the hour of the day at which the view it taken.' For Talbot the prospect was opened up of seeing the world in different ways. In a prophetic insight, Talbot saw photography as an extension of vision when he postulated the use of 'certain invisible rays which lie beyond the violet, and beyond the limits of the spectrum . . . to fill a room . . . The eye of the camera would see plainly where the human eye would find nothing but darkness.' Talbot went on to say: 'Alas! that this speculation is somewhat too refined to be introduced into a modern novel or romance.'[62] But today we have infra red and ultra violet photography which allow the camera to produce images from beyond both ends of the visible spectrum. Talbot's passion for recording information stretched even into his portraits and groups which might be thought to be above his utilitarian instincts. He notes that 'Portraits of living persons and groups of figures form one of the most attractive subjects of photography', and later records: 'I have observed that family groups are especial favourites.' Yet almost immediately the functional view comes through: 'What would be the value to our English Nobility of such a record of their ancestors who lived a century ago? On how small a portion of their familiar picture gallery can they rely with confidence.'[63] That complex detail could be recorded with such an economy of labour was a characteristic of photography which impressed Talbot from the very beginning. In his 1839 paper he recorded that the first kind of objects he attempted to copy were flowers and leaves and these were rendered 'with the utmost truth and fidelity, exhibiting even the venation of the leaves, the minute hairs that clothe the plant, etc. . . . The object which would take the most skilful artist days or weeks of labour to trace or to copy, is effected by the boundless powers of natural chemistry in the space of a few seconds.'[64] The detail recorded on a daguerreotype plate was far superior to anything that could be recorded on paper and this must have impressed Talbot as much as it impressed his contemporaries. It would have certainly suggested to Talbot that his process was capable of improvement and in much of his work he was striving to capture more and more detail. When discussing *The Pencil of Nature,* the correspondent of *The Athenaeum* spoke in comparative terms of the 'broad and massive studies by Rembrandt', and compared them with 'the microscopic imitations of many of the Dutch painters'.[65] Perhaps Talbot's familiarity with the Dutch school extended to admiration and he was always striving to achieve their detail. If this was the case, then it must have been a disappointment for him that he was only equipped with the tools to produce a Rembrandt. There were others, however, who were to exploit just those characteristics Talbot sought to refine. They were so successful that just ten years later when the calotype process was, to all intents and purposes, finished, *The Quarterly Review* looked back with nostalgia: 'But let us examine a little more closely those advances which photography owes to science — we mean in an artistic sense. We turn to the portraits, our premiers amours, now taken under every appliance of facility both for sitter and operator. Far greater detail and precision accordingly appear . . .

what was at first only suggestion is now all careful making out, — but the likeness to Rembrandt and Reynolds is gone! There is no mystery in this . . .'[66] It is doubtful if Talbot applauded this sentiment, even if he regretted the passing of his process. His whole life was dedicated to providing explanations of the mysterious.

Talbot's last scientific notebook stops on 23 April 1843. For some reason he did not start another but recorded his notes on loose sheets which are difficult to collate and assess. It is unlikely that he immediately stopped work on his photographic process but there can be little doubt that from about this time it tailed off quite rapidly. He seems to have continued to take photographs himself only until about 1846 or 1847. Although he lived for another thirty years, apart from a very few specialised experimental images, no surviving photographs can be positively attributed to Talbot after 1847. There must, therefore, be a strong suspicion that his prime interest in photography was in solving the technical problems. Talbot was first and foremost a scientist and for him the great attraction of photography was the scientists' satisfaction in harnessing nature to provide a completely unique and original invention. Talbot was under no illusions that he had refined the art to a definitive form. The 'Introductory Remarks' to The Pencil of Nature contain a message of explanation and apology. He asks that the readers 'excuse the imperfections necessarily incident to a first attempt to exhibit an Art of so great singularity, which employs processes entirely new, and having no analogy to any thing in use before. That such imperfections will occur in a first essay, must indeed be expected. At present the Art can hardly be said to have advanced beyond its infancy'. Talbot had set the infant on its first faltering steps but was happy to let others see it through the trials of adolescence. During the 1840s Talbot continued to support Henneman, at first at the Reading establishment, and later in a London studio in Regent Street. He corresponded regularly with friends such as the Rev. Calvert Jones, and the Rev. George Bridges who had learned their photography from him and arranged for Henneman to produce prints from their negatives. In 1851 Talbot made the first high-speed flash photograph when he recorded the revolving pages of a newspaper in about 1/100,000 of a second using the spark form a battery as a light source. During the 1850s he evolved the first practical system of photo-engraving.

Talbot's title of 'Father of Photography' was earned for his invention of the negative-positive process but it is deserved for another reason. Most of the early photographers saw photography as painting in another medium, and accordingly produced photographs which used the conventions of established art. Talbot had the breadth of vision to see that his new art offered different opportunities, a new view of the physical world around him. For him, photography was a working tool, an invaluable means of duplicating and multiplying images, and a unique recording system. Almost alone, he saw photography as it is practised today. Talbot died at Lacock on 16 September 1877. His obituaries were fulsome and generous; they appeared in all the leading newspapers and scientific journals of the day. But he would probably have been satisfied with the first lines of the notice in his local Wiltshire Telegraph: 'There was laid in the grave in the pretty cemetery of this parish yesterday, one of whom it may be said that he was the originator of one of the most wonderful discoveries of the present age.'[67]

NOTES

1. H. Fox Talbot, The Pencil of Nature, 1844-46.
2. Ibid.
3. For an account of the English landed classes in the 19th century see F. M. L. Thompson, English Landed Society in the Nineteenth Century, Routledge and Kegan Paul, 1971.

4. D. S. L. Cartwell, *The Organisation of Science in England,* Heinemann revised paperback edition, 1972, p.54.
5. Compiled from lists of published papers and patents in H. J. P. Arnold, *William Henry Fox Talbot,* Hutchinson Benham, 1977.
6. According to Marjorie Hope Nicolson, *Newton Demands the Muse,* Princeton University Press, 1946.
7. H. Fox Talbot, op. cit.
8. H. F. Talbot, 'Some Account of the Art of Photogenic Drawing', *Philosophical Magazine,* XIV, 1839, pp.196-208.
9. H. Fox Talbot, op. cit.
10. 'Some Account of the Art of Photogenic Drawing', op. cit. p.205.
11. Ibid, pp.207-208.
12. *The Mechanics Magazine,* No. 809, 9 February 1839, p.328.
13. *The Magazine of Science,* No. 3, 20 April 1839, p.18.
14. *The Mirror,* No. 945, 20 April 1829, p.242.
15. *The Mirror,* No. 946, 27 April 1839, p.262.
16. See *The Magazine of Science,* No. 4, 27 April 1839.
17. *The Mechanics Magazine,* No. 816, 30 March 1839, p.455.
18. Fox Talbot Museum, ms. letter, Lady Theresa Digby to Talbot, 13 April 1839.
19. Fox Talbot Museum, ms. LA 39-43 letter, G. Butler to Talbot, 31 May 1839.
20. Fox Talbot Museum, ms. letter, C. R. M. Talbot to Talbot, 30 March 1839.
21. *The Mechanics Magazine,* No. 815, 23 March 1839, p.447.
22. *The Mirror,* No. 947, 4 May 1839, p.283.
23. Andrew Fyfe, 'On Photography', *Edinburgh New Philosophical Journal,* Vol. 27, 1839. pp.144-155.
24. Robert Hunt, *A Popular Treatise on the Art of Photography,* Introduction, 1841.
25. Science Museum, ms. letter, Herschel to Talbot, 9 May 1839.
26. Science Museum, ms. notebook 'P', 6 February 1839 to 25 June 1840.
27. A printed sheet listing all the photogenic drawings displayed was produced for the meeting. There are copies in both the Science Museum and the Fox Talbot Museum collections.
28. Fox Talbot Museum, ms. LA 39-51 letter, Lady Elisabeth to Talbot, (?) October 1839.
29. *The Literary Gazette,* No. 1217, 16 May 1840, p.315.
30. Ibid.
31. Quoted by Arnold, op. cit.
32. Science Museum, ms. notebook 'Q', 26 June 1840 to 23 April 1843.
33. Robert Graham, 'The Early History of Photography,' *Good Words,* 1874, pp.450-451.
34. Science Museum, ms. notebook 'Q'.
35. Patent No. 9753, *Photography,* 1 June 1843.
36. Fox Talbot Museum, ms. LA 42-64 letter, C. R. M. Talbot to Talbot, 24 August(?) 1842.
37. Fox Talbot Museum, ms. LA 42-64 letter, W. H. Furlong to Talbot, March 1843.
38. George Cundell, 'On the Practice of the Calotype Process of Photography,' *Philosophical Magazine,* XLVIII, 1844, p.321.
39. *British Journal of Photography,* 5 August 1864, p.279.
40. Fox Talbot Museum, ms. LA 41-60 letter, Lady Mary Cole to Talbot, 4 October 1841.
41. Fox Talbot Museum, ms. LA 41-60 letter, William Fox Strangways to Talbot, 2 November 1841.
42. Science Museum, ms. letter, Herschel to Talbot, 21 April 1842.
43. *The Chemist,* Vol. III, 1842, p.122
44. From a printed publication notice advertising Part I of *The Pencil of Nature.* There are several copies in the Science Museum collection.
45. *Quarterly Review,* No. 101, 1857, p.461.
46. *The Art Union,* 1 June 1846, p.143.
47. Isaac Newton's paper, *'Opticks: Or a Treatise on the Reflections, Refractions, Inflections and Colours of Light'* was first published in 1704 although it was a compilation of work carried out over a period of more than thirty years.
48. Part of an 'Epitaph intended for Sir Isaac Newton' by Alexander Pope. Quoted by Nicolson, op. cit.
49. From Keats *Lamia II.* Quoted by Nicolson, op. cit.
50. From William Paley, *Natural Theology, 1802, Chapter 21, (IV).*
51. *Quoted by Anne Treneer, The Mercurial Chemist,* 1963, p.35.
52. *The Literary Gazette,* 2 February 1839, p.74. Quoted by Arnold, op. cit.
53. H. Fox Talbot, op. cit. notes to Plate III.
54. Hunt, op. cit.
55. Thomas Carlyle, *Signs of the Times,* 1829.
56. *The Art Union,* 1 March 1848.
57. H. Fox Talbot, op. cit. notes to Plate VI.
58. *The Photographic Journal,* 15 November 1860, p.33.
59. *The Art Union,* June 1848, p.238.
60. Quoted by Arnold, op. cit. p.132.
61. H. Fox Talbot, op. cit. notes to Plate I.
62. Ibid, notes to Plate VIII.
63. Ibid, notes to Plate XIV.
64. 'Some Account of the Art of Photogenic Drawing', op. cit., Plate 99.
65. *The Athenaeum,* No. 985, 12 September 1846, p.939.
66. *The Quarterly Review.* No. 101, 1857, p.461.
67. *The Wiltshire Telegraph,* 22 September 1877.

16 DETAIL FROM AN ENGRAVING BY
JOSEPH EBSWORTH, SHOWING THE
DAGUERREOTYPE PHOTOGRAPHER,
JAMES HOWIE, OPERATING ON A ROOF
TOP.
Drawn from the Scott Monument

ROBERT ADAMSON AND DAVID OCTAVIUS HILL

On 9 May 1843, Sir David Brewster wrote to William Henry Fox Talbot: 'Mr. Adamson, of whom I have previously written to you, goes tomorrow to Edinr. to prosecute, as a Profession, the calotype. He has made brilliant progress and done some of the very finest things both in Portrait and Landscape. His Risk & outlay are considerable; & he is therefore anxious to make a good beginning. For this purpose he is desirous that you would allow him to state that he practises the art with your concurrence and countenance.'[68]

Robert Adamson had been taught the calotype process by his older brother, Dr. John Adamson. Sir David Brewster had in the previous three years corresponded at great length with Talbot, gradually drawing from him the details of the process and encouraging his friends in St. Andrews, Major Playfair and Dr. Adamson, in their laborious and frequently unsuccessful experiments. In May 1842, John Adamson succeeded in taking the first portrait calotype in Scotland and from that point the St. Andrews circle appears to have mastered the process. Robert Adamson had been training to be an engineer but his health was poor and he was persuaded to take up photography as a career instead.

Part of Robert Adamson's outlay was the rent of Rock House. This small terrace house, which is the highest private house on Calton Hill below a cluster of public buildings, was very well placed to act as a studio. The portrait photographs were taken in a walled garden which gave Robert Adamson an immediate advantage over the other professional photographers. Most of the early 'studios' in cities were roof-tops and the photographer's clients were obliged to labour up narrow flights of stairs and clamber onto roofs to sit among the chimney pots in the sunshine. James Howie, a daguerreotypist working in Princes Street, had such an arrangement: 'His sitters had to climb three flights of stairs, and then by a kind of ladder reached a skylight, through which they got access to the roof of the house. The posing-chair, with something in the shape of a headrest fixed to its back, was placed against the gable of the adjoining building, and the operator used to take the sitter by the shoulders and press him down with the observation — "There! now sit still as death!"'[69] (Fig 16).

Even safely on ground level, the opportunities for farce were considerable. On windy days in Edinburgh, small boys could make a respectable living from chasing top hats. James Good Tunny's account of early photography records: 'I remember my old friend Thomas Davidson having constructed a new lens. Sir David Brewster and two other scientific friends were at the testing of it, when it was resolved that they should adjourn to the space of ground now occupied by the East Prince's Gardens. Mr. Howie's camera stand was rather ricketty, so a large window or clock weight always accompanied it. One of Sir David's friends was placed on a chair in the best light — in fact, with the full blaze of the sun in his face. Mr. Howie got his camera focussed, and the clock weight laid on the top of his camera to keep it steady, and was just about to draw up the slide when his sitter began to mutter something about his hat going to be blown away, when old Howie at once satisfied him that there would be little danger of it moving far, as he, with the rough exclamation of " — your hat," at once transfixed it with the clock weight. The exposure being over, the gentleman found his hat thoroughly ventilated, as the clock weight had passed right through the crown!'[70] The long-faced melancholy of many Victorian photographs has more than one explanation.

By contrast, Robert Adamson was working safely on the ground in a sheltered garden nearly 100 metres above sea level.

It is difficult to judge which of the calotypes were taken by Robert Adamson within the two or three weeks of May when he was working alone. Surprisingly, he does not seem to have advertised his arrival and it was not noted in the newspapers. He may have spent these weeks substantially in organising the studio and settling in.

Sir David Brewster, keeping an eye on his protégé, took the first opportunity to send business his way. By a fortunate chance, this business was brought by the painter, David Octavius Hill.

D. O. Hill had been swept up in a wave of unparalleled enthusiasm which struck Edinburgh on 18 May 1843. A dispute within the Church of Scotland, centring on the right of the owners of presentations to livings to put in ministers against the will of the Church Presbyteries had reached a legal deadlock. On 18 May, when the General Assembly of the Church opened, the party within the Church which supported the Presbyteries' right of veto, led by the Moderator himself, uttered a formal protest and then rose and abandoned the Assembly.

The strength of feeling behind this gesture — when more than a third of the ministers walked out — was immense. The ministers were walking out of the Church itself, away from their livings, and, in the words of Lord Cockburn, 'They have abandoned that public station which was the ambition of their lives, and have descended from certainty to precariousness, and most of them, from comfort to destitution, solely for their principles . . .'[71] The emotional feeling of the party was expressed by the Rev. Dr. Stewart of Cromarty who said, 'When I read that interdict by a Civil Court, which the Church was called and commanded to obey (overruling the Presbyteries' objections), I felt as I could imagine a child to feel hanging at the breast of its mother, if that mother had been suddenly shot through the heart. I might cling to the body but the life has gone out of her.'[72]

This revolution in the Church strongly affected the bystanders. D. O. Hill was sufficiently moved to wish to paint a great history picture to commemorate the occasion and his enthusiasm was underlined by Lord Cockburn who applauded the project: 'There has not been such a subject since the days of Knox — and not then!'[73]

Hill gained permission to draw the proceedings from the best viewpoint and apparently began to paint individual portrait sketches (Catalogue 173-5) in intervals between the Assembly sessions. Six days after the Disruption he was advertising engravings from the picture, which he estimated would be ready in two to three years.

Sir David Brewster who had a prominent role in the new Free Church took an interest also in Hill's painting. At some point before 9 June, he 'got hold of the Artist — showed him the Calotype, & the immediate advantage he might derive from it in getting likenesses of all the principal characters before they dispersed to their respective homes. He was at first incredulous, but went to Mr. Adamson, and arranged with him preliminaries for getting all the necessary portraits'.[74] Hill's scepticism was not proof against Brewster's enthusiasm and it was possibly only politeness which drove him up to Rock House in the first instance.

Within a couple of weeks, in which Hill invited the ministers to sit for group and individual portraits, he had learned enough about the calotype process to change his attitude to it entirely. The early groups and portraits were taken solely in terms of their usefulness to the painting — backgrounds ignored and supports in full view (Catalogue 178). It is a measure of Hill's sudden excitement about the calotype that he was distracted away from this purely practical exercise by realising the possibilities opened up by the process. For him to be distracted from his great historical picture before he had even properly started on it, is astonishing.

Brewster's letter to Talbot, dated 3 July, continued: 'They have succeeded beyond their most sanguine expectations. — They have taken on a small scale, Groups of 25 persons in the same picture all placed in attitudes which the Painter desired, and very large Pictures besides have been taken of each individual to assist the Painter in the completion of his picture.

Mr. D. O. Hill, the Painter, is on the eve of entering into partnership with Mr. Adamson and proposes to apply the Calotype to many other general purposes of a very popular kind, & especially to the execution of large pictures representing difft. bodies & classes of individuals.

I think you will find that we have, in Scotland, found out the value of your invention not before yourself, but before those to whom you have given the privilege of using it.'[74]

On 8 July Hill and Adamson advertised an exhibition in Alexander Hill's Galleries in Princes Street. This was to be 'Mr. D. O. Hill's Picture of the First General Assembly of the Free Protesting Church of Scotland.

A large number of the preliminary Studies and Sketches for the above National Picture, as also of a projected Series of Portraits of Clergymen and Laymen of the Free Protesting Church of Scotland, comprising nearly the whole of the Calotype Pictures executed jointly by Mr. ADAMSON and Mr. HILL, will be exhibited Privately at Mr. A. Hill's Galleries 67 Princes Street On Wednesday 12th inst, and following week'.[75]

This advertisement shows that they were already thinking of the calotypes as independent from the painting, and the photographic 'sketches' had become a 'projected series of portraits'. Brewster's letter suggests that they had a whole range of projects already in mind. One of the people involved in the early calotyping sessions was Hugh Miller, the journalist (Catalogue 113), who must have been present during the early discussions at Rock House. He published an article on 'The Calotype' in *The Witness* newspaper on 12 July which presumably expresses some of the ideas Hill and Adamson had in mind. The calotype was, he said, 'A real invention, which bids fair to produce some of the greatest revolutions in the fine arts of which they have ever been the subject . . . The connoisseur unacquainted with the results of the recent discovery, would decide, if shown a set of photographic impressions, that he had before him the carefully finished drawings in sepia of some great master.' He discussed the ideas raised by the calotype at length:

'One result of the discovery of the calotype will be, we doubt not, the production of completer treatises on perspective than have yet been given to the world. Another very curious result will be, in all probability, a new mode of design for the purposes of the engraver, especially for all the illustrations of books. For a large class of works the labours of the artist bid fair to be restricted to the composition of *tableaux vivants*, which it will be the part of the photographer to fix, and then transfer to the engraver. . . In glancing over the photographic sketches, one cannot avoid being struck by the silent but impressive eulogium which nature pronounces, through their agency, on the works of the more eminent masters. There is much in seeing nature truthfully, and in registering what are really her prominent markings. Artists of a lower order are continually falling into mere mannerisms, there is an eye of fresh observation required — that ability of continuous attention to surrounding phenomena which only superior men possess; and doubtless to this eye of fresh observation, this ability of continuous attention, the masters owed much of their truth and their power. How very truthfully and perseveringly some of them saw, is well illustrated by these photographic drawings. Here, for instance, is a portrait exactly after the manner of Raeburn. There is the same broad freedom of touch ... here is another portrait, quiet, deeply-toned, gentlemanly, — a transcript apparently of one of the more characteristic portraits of Sir Thomas Lawrence. Perhaps, however, of all our British artists, the artist whose published works most nearly resemble a set of these drawings is Sir Joshua Reynolds.'

Miller made further points — one which has already been expressed by Sir David Brewster (Catalogue 108) that portraits of one person taken from different angles at different times may differ considerably in appearance, and the other based on Dr. Thomas Brown's 'theory of attention' by which objects may be seen without being *looked at.* Miller concluded, examining the appearance of the calotype — focussed in the centre, unfocussed at the edges — that this was a purely optical effect. 'The subject', Miller said, 'is so suggestive of thought at the present stage, that it would be no easy matter to exhaust it; and it will, we have no doubt, be still more suggestive of thought by and by.'[76]

Miller's opinions must come substantially from Hill and Adamson and are probably mostly echoes of Hill. The astonishment, the sense of great future potential, and the belief that the calotype would cause revolutions in the fine arts, must be a direct reflection of Hill's own feelings at the time — the very reasons he joined in partnership with Adamson.

The practical working of the partnership can be pieced together from different sources. James Good Tunny recalled more than thirty years later that 'Hill and Adamson's calotype portraits became the wonder of every gathering of scientific or artistic men. Time after time have I gone and stood on the projecting rock below Playfair's monument on Calton Hill, and drawn inspiration from viewing Mr. Adamson placing a large square box upon a stand, covering his head with a focussing-cloth, introducing the slide, counting the seconds by his watch, putting the cap on the lens, and retiring to what we now know to be the dark room. Oh! if I could only have got an introduction to these men, it would have been the consummation of my happiness! But it was destined that I should continue to work unaided in my experiments for a considerable time.'[77]

Hill himself was clearly not present all the time. He was officially the Secretary of the Royal Scottish Academy and by profession a landscape painter, though his painting suffered during the years he was interested in the calotype. More surprising, Adamson was sometimes absent. He was away for the winter months of 1843 to 1844. Both men had bouts of sickness which also prevented them from working at times. Their joint output of 3,000 images between 1843 and 1847 is all the more astonishing. It is partly explained by their assistant or assistants. The King of Saxony's travelling party visited Rock House unexpectedly in 1844 and found that, 'Unfortunately the master himself was not in the way, and an assistant was obliged to conduct the process. The result was not very successful'.[78]

This, or a later assistant, is first named in a letter from James Nasmyth to Hill in April 1845 which also contains one of the few references to Robert Adamson himself: 'Pray present my best regards to that authentic and worthy person Mr. Adamson. He is of rare merit and most praisworthy perseverence, not forgetting Miss Mann. The sisterhood [illegible] their very kindest regards to her, not forgetting yourself.'[79]

Miss Mann was still working at Rock House in March 1847 when a later letter from Nasmyth enquired, 'how goes on the divine solar art? and how does that worthy artist Mr. Adamson the authentic contriver & manipulator in the art of light and darkness? and thrice worthy Miss Mann that most skillfull and zealous of assistants. You must excuse me bothering you with so many questions of that kind as I have the remembrance of all on Em [of them] so clearly calotyped in my minds Eye as last I saw them in full manipulation of the divine art of light—'.[80]

Hill's role in the partnership was 'purely that of an artist. I know not the process though it is done under my nose continually and I believe I never will'.[81] It fell to him to organise and direct the sitters, background and lighting, while Adamson undertook the chemistry and manipulation.

Robert Adamson apparently had three cameras when he first arrived in Edinburgh — he left John Adamson without a camera at all. The calotypes taken by these cameras varied in size from the original small square photographs to the $8\frac{1}{2} \times 6\frac{1}{2}$ inch size. Hill rejected the smallest size fairly rapidly and the intermediate size probably after a month or two, although it was still used occasionally for basic studio portraiture. These cameras were probably all made by the Edinburgh instrument maker and daguerreotypist, Thomas Davidson, who was supplying cameras to the St. Andrews circle. In 1844 they acquired a far bigger camera. Hill was requested to send a group of the calotypes to the first exhibition of the Photographic Society of Scotland in 1856 and wrote to the Secretary: 'I hope to be able to send some time today a frame with two or three calotypes done by us a very long time ago — of a size 16 inches by 14 & under, when there were no other calotypes in existence even half of the same size. Considering the size — the period & that they were from an Edinburgh made camera — they may also possess an interest to a Scottish Photographic Society as enabling them to claim for Scotland an honorable priority in certain phases of the art'.[82]

Thomas Davidson talked about the big camera in 1859: 'Messrs Adamson and Hill, already alluded to, had also a camera, about two feet square, fitted up for taking portraits as large as life; but the imperfections in it, & difficulty of preparing paper so large, were against it. I also made a speculum of 24" diameter & 30" focus, for the aforesaid, for taking smaller portraits, or to reflect light on the object; but that was never much used.'[83]

The camera was apparently adaptable and could either take photographs 16×13 inches using a lens, or a smaller size, $11\frac{3}{4} \times 10\frac{1}{2}$ or $11\frac{3}{4} \times 9$ inches using a mirror. The larger size was used only for architecture presumably because the lens only took long exposures. The idea of using a mirror instead of a lens to circumvent the aberrations in the lens and to reduce the exposure time had first been patented in America by Alexander Wolcott and John Johnson, and through their agency it was patented in England by Richard Beard in 1840. It was apparently not patented in Scotland. In the Wolcott-Johnson camera the light from the subject passed into the camera through a large hole in the front to a curved mirror at the back which collected the light and focussed it on the sensitised plate held in a plate holder in the centre of the camera. As it was originally worked out, the camera was used for the daguerreotype process and took a small photograph using a large camera. Thomas Davidson's version of this was proposing to take a comparatively large photograph by the paper process.

Davidson supplied Rock House with another piece of equipment. He wrote: 'It is now more than sixteen years since I assisted Messrs. Adamson & Hill, photographers, Edinburgh, in taking a few copies of magnified representations of minute objects by an achromatic solar microscope, which I had made for Mr. Octavius David Hill, Calton Stairs, Edinburgh. (At that time the calotype paper was employed, & of course the outline was not so well defined as with Collodion on glass, the latter process not being then known). The objects I adopted were transverse sections of wood, abour $\frac{3}{8}''$ in diameter.

The enlarged copies were, so far as I recollect, about 18″ in diameter. The last time I saw the aforesaid magnified impressions, they were framed & hanging in James Bryson's shop, Princes Street, Edinburgh; & as regards patents, Mr. Hill & Mr. Adamson had arranged to lodge a *Caveat,* but the premature & lamented death of the latter prevented it.'[84] Photographs had been taken through a solar microscope before — by Talbot amongst others — so it is not clear what they were thinking of patenting. Regrettably neither the instrument nor its prints have been found. The interesting point here is that Adamson, who is known as a chemist, and Hill, who is known as an artist, had an idea between them about solar microscopes which the instrument-maker himself was prepared to regard as their patent.

By the end of 1843, Sir David Brewster was reporting to Talbot on the progress of the calotype in Scotland: 'I wish I could send you some of the fine Calotypes of ancient Church yard Monuments, as well as modern ones taken by Mr. Adamson, and also specimens of the fine groups of Picturesque personages which Mr. Hill and he have arranged and photo-graphed. Those of the Fishermen & women of Newhaven are singularly excellent. They have been so inundated with work that they have not been able to send me a Collection which they have promised. I think your plan of publication excellent. The same idea had occurred to Mr. Hill & Mr. Adamson, who advertised it some time ago as a plan in contemplation.

Mr. Adamson and Mr. Hill get up all their calotypes by cutting off the black border, and attaching them to Bristol Board . . .'[85]

Three calotypes taken in Greyfriars' Churchyard are dated August and September 1843 and these are probably part of a group of photographs of the churchyard commissioned by the painter, George Harvey, responding to Hill's idea that the calotype could be applied 'especially to the execution of large pictures . . .' In the event, Harvey found himself unable to use the photographs.

In October they had attended the second meeting of the Free Church in Glasgow where they were able to take more calotypes for the Disruption Picture.

In November there is further evidence that the painters were taking a close interest in Rock House. The watercolourist John Harden wrote to his daughters: 'I have sat and stood for a likeness & hope it will be approved of. Sir Wm. Allan arranged my standing attitude'.[86] Allan was the President of the Royal Scottish Academy and is quoted by Hill in 1845 as an enthusiast for the calotype (Catalogue 128).

At the end of the year, the excellence of Hill and Adamson's work received public recognition. They exhibited in the Board of Manufactures' exhibition and were awarded a prize of ten pounds, for 'combining in the happiest possible manner artistical freedom of excellence with scientific precision of execution'.[87]

Calotype photography was a seasonal profession and Robert Adamson seems to have left Edinburgh in mid-November and not to have returned until mid-April 1844. The first dated negative for the year is 20 April and David Brewster refers to his absence in a letter dated 18 April: 'I gave your request, as I think I wrote you, to Dr. Adamson for his brother, along with the calotypes you were so good as to send him. This delay in writing you, has arisen from his having left Edinr. about the time you wrote me, & from his desire to send you one or two good negatives for your work. Dr. Adamson is so annoyed at the circumstance that he has got my camera, for the purpose of getting one or two good negatives for you, so I hope the oversight will be atoned for.'[88]

Assuming Robert Adamson to have gone back to St. Andrews for the winter, he did not take a camera with him and was apparently not taking photographs for four months.

Hill, who had been living in Inverleith Row to the north of Princes Street, moved into Rock House at about this time, and the calotype operations took on a new momentum. They acquired the big camera before 13 June (the first dated negative), and in August were advertising six volumes of calotypes. These were to be 'in a style of great elegance on a paper the size and quality of "Roberts' Views in the Holy Land"'[89] and the subjects were *The Fishermen and Women of the Firth of Forth, Highland Character and Costume, The Architectural Structures of Edinburgh, The Architectural Structures of Glasgow, &c, Old Castles, Abbeys &c in Scotland,* and *Portraits of Distinguished Scotchmen.* These were to sell at a price of five guineas each. Unfortunately, this project came to nothing, although Hill makes a passing reference to the first in a letter in Spring 1845: 'We are preparing Fishwives for a book . . .'[90]

During 1844, Hill and Adamson took their most interesting group of large photographs at Merchiston Castle School, where the Rev. Dr. Thomas Chalmers's brother, Charles, was headmaster. They apparently took over the school and its grounds for at least a day to take photographs of the Chalmers family as well as crowd scenes of the schoolboys (Catalogue 150 and 196).

The calotypes were on exhibition early in 1844 in Cupar in Fife.[91] St. Andrews itself as a University town was hostile to dissent and the Disruption and indeed tried to oust Sir David Brewster for his connection with the Free Church. Cupar as the nearest substantial independent town to St. Andrews could take the calotype studies for the Disruption Picture without entering into acrimonious debate with the St. Andrews establishment. The same or an extended exhibition of about two hundred photographs was sent to Liverpool in September, where it was on view at Mr. Grundy's Repository of the Arts.[92]

Also in September, the Académie des Sciences in Paris were shown a large collection of the calotypes carried over by Alexander Christie, the Director of the Ornamental Department of the Trustees' Academy in Edinburgh. The painter, Ary Scheffer, was apparently impressed but the report of the meeting suggests that the Académie preferred the daguerreotype process.

At the end of the month, Hill wrote a formal letter to Talbot requesting his permission to take calotypes at the British Association in York, which was covered by the English patent: 'It has been suggested to Mr. Adamson and myself, to attend the meeting of the British Association at York for the purpose of making Calotype Portraits of some of the eminent men who may be present.'[93] The British Association meetings were three-yearly international conferences for exchange of scientific information, and were as natural an opportunity for Hill and Adamson to take a series of portraits of important scientists, as the Free Church meetings which enabled them to gather distinguished churchmen. It may have been Brewster, a leading figure in the Association, who made the suggestion.

Hill and Adamson took the big and the standard size cameras to York. Their photography achieved only mixed success. Technically there were too many failures and the atmosphere at York was critical in the extreme. Four papers given at the meeting were descriptions of different photographic processes by Professor Robert Hunt, Sir John Herschel, Professor William Grove and Dr. Thomas Woods. Talbot himself spent the meeting attacking the originality of these processes in defence of the calotype and left York in a state of severe strain. Hill felt similar antagonism, 'though a few of them [the calotypes] were among the best things I have tried'. Two of their more splendid architectural photographs, York Minster and Durham Cathedral (Catalogue 189 and 190) were taken on this occasion and were applauded by Lady Eastlake: '. . . one of Durham most exquisite',[94] and James Nasmyth: '. . . that Durham and York Minster! its sure they are noble very *pitch* forks of art to set me a [illegible] on the right key at once. It is nature reduced to an artistical standard and abounding in the most noble suggestion'.[95]

At the end of October, Hill's involvement in photography was noted at a public dinner for Dr. William Pyper. One of Hill's friends, John Thomson Gordon, gave a speech which included this passage: 'He did not wish to particularize individuals, but in proposing a bumper to the Scottish Academy, he might be allowed to join with it the name of his excellent friend Mr. Hill, whose brush had often been dipped in the sunbeam, but who now painted with the sunbeam itself. (This allusion to Mr. Hill's novel application of the calotype to artistic purposes was received with great applauses)'.[96]

Despite the enthusiasm of his friends, Hill was beginning to feel concerned about his involvement in photography. He sent a portfolio of the calotypes to Dominic Colnaghi in London at the beginning of 1845 and wrote to David Roberts that he should choose any he wanted. In 1849 when three volumes of the calotypes were being specially bound by Colnaghis, for the Royal Academy, Roberts recalled, 'But a few years back the *same parties* endeavoured to *burke* [conceal] a Portfolio of the very same caliotypes, intrusted to their care — by throwing them under the counter instead of on it . . .'[97] Roberts carried off the whole portfolio and Hill responded:

'By all means make any use of the portfolio of Calotypes which you think may in any way gratify yourself or any of your friends. They are altogether at your service to appropriate or not, and I must feel highly pleased that you think them worthy of being shewn at the Graphic Society as at Lord Northampton's. His Lordship I had the honour to Calotype at York, and succeeded in making what I think a singularly Rembrantish & very fine study. I did a few other things at York — which by the Yorkites have since been considered beastly affairs (though a few of them were among the best things I have tried) but one Yorkites opinion consoles me — for *Etty* saw in them revivals of Rembrant Titian and Spagnoletto. A little more of the Calotype in the Spring months & in all probability I will then leave it to be worked out by less occupied hands'.[98]

The note of depression and the desire to withdraw from photography were overtaken in Hill's next letter to Roberts, two weeks later. This is the most important, as well as the most enthusiastic of Hill's letters about the calotype and also the most strikingly illegible.

Hill explains this in the following letter: 'Before I dispatched my letter of the 12th to you, Adamson had subjected it to the process of being copied by putting it through a press — which made such a mess of the original, that my always illegible hand, was nearly if not wholly obliterated. I fear in truth that it would defy your intelligence to make out.'[99]

It reinforces the interest of this letter that Hill was prepared to send it in this condition and that for once we can be certain that Hill was expressing not just his own but also Robert Adamson's enthusiasm and opinions:

'I cannot fail to be more than gratified by the intelligence I received from you this morning as to the manner in which the portfolio of our Calotypes had been received by yourself, by Stanfield, and the distinguished guests of Lord Northampton. Your flattering opinions have been shared by Etty Allan Leitch and many artists and a few [illegible] who know what art is, and these I have used as a warm blanket, to restore me to my natural heat, after a few cold bucketings of ignorant criticism, which my desire to foster and improve this hand maiden of Fine Art, has exposed me to. Most welcome therefore and highly prized by me are Stanfield's and your own cordial approval of our labour. Accept of my gratitude both of you.

Adamson in answer to some of your queries respecting this Photogenic Process.

The Art is the invention of Mr. Fox Talbot who is the sole patentee: his patent extends in England only. About three years ago this said process was chemically and artistically speaking a very miserable affair. Dr. Adamson of St. Andrews — brother of my friend R. Adamson whose manipulation produced the pictures now with you, took up Mr. Talbot's process as an amateur. You are aware how jealous some scientific men are, as to their rights in the paternity of inventions or improvements, therefore I say *entre nous* that I believe Dr. Adamson & his brother to be the fathers of many of these parts of the process which make it a valuable and practical art. I believe also from all I have seen that Robert Adamson is the most successful manipulator the art has yet seen, and his steady industry and knowledge of chemistry, is such that both from him and his brother much new improvements may yet be expected. I must tell you that Dr. Adamson, up to the time that his brother thought of using the art professionally, was a most liberal communicator to all and every one, of all his improvements — and Mr. Talbot had regularly a knowledge of his results. Mr. Talbots patent not withstanding Adamsons improvements of his processes you will thus see prevent us from executing, or at least, selling a work in England without his consent. Some days ago I wrote for this to Mr. Talbot — a few days will l hope tell me with what success. You have cracked the very kernal of my desire in reference to a work of Calotypes — my ambition is to leave my name on a great and noble work worthy of England and of this *English* invention — and it has often appeared to me possible nay probable and most seemly that the Queen of England — and the leading nobles would patronise a work of this nature — a noble and worthy launch in the eyes of the Arts of Europe of a great English discovery — But the very excellence of the art exhibited in the Calotype is a bar to its popularity with the unlearned public — it is absolutely necessary to success, that means may be taken by those who have the power to get the scheme backed by the names of those entitled to lead in taste and in patronage. The means you have already taken my dear Roberts may, if the things are worthy, do much — and of the interest excited at Lord Northampton's — could be extended to Windsor — to Peel — Aberdeen — Lord Lansdowne Sutherland ['Egerton' crossed out] &c &c there could be little danger of a worthy result. I, though much occupied would have no hesitation in undertaking to conduct a work of this sort of British statesmen and others — provided I was backed in such a high quarter as would command the necessary sittings from the personages to be represented. I am somewhat ambitious in the sort of book I would like to give myself to in bringing out — and would look for something in splendour of *bringing out,* like to your wonderful efforts in bookmaking — I don't say in extent — but I say that this first book of English Calotype *pictures* for really Talbot's examples in his Pencil of Nature are not intended to be such should be such as to make the French look only second best in their Sun Painting efforts. It should almost be a book worthy of the tables [?] of sovereigns and of the highest cognoscenti. Now there is my naked bosom in the matter, which I hope will not make you rate me as absolute and arragant as Petruccio making you exclaim. "Why! This gallant will command the sun." You ask, "Can it be kept secret." I can only say that Adamson says the manipulation is very liable to go wrong in the hands of most people — that tho' several have now and then produced a good specimen — they find it difficult to succeed often — and the arrangement of the picture is as much an effort of the artist as if he was in reality going to paint it (This last of course to ['be' missing?] understood with its necessary limitations.) I [illegible] therefore that in the common acceptation of the word it cannot be called secret — tho Adamson thinks he knows some things others do not.

My connection with the art has been purely that of an artist. I know not the process though it is done under my nose continually and I believe I never will. Until I took it up the best things I saw — were, though chemically fine — artistically nothing. Were we in London I doubt not I might make an arrangement with Mons Allen [? Claudet]. If a volume or two of these were published they would cost about 5/ a plate — they are sold at 7/6 separately — that is those we sell. I would that you took in the meantime possession of the whole portfolio. Tell Colnaghi you have my order to do so — shewing them to such of your friends and the friends of Art, as it might be desireable to impress favourably with the art. Could a work of 100 200 or 300 subjects not succeed at the prices I have named 30 40 or 50 subscribers would lay the expense and labour, if more were sold, some reward might accrue.

Let me have your thoughts on this subject, and should anything I have written appear to you absurd and [illegible] do not let my self opinionated expressions however strongly urged come between me and the true report of your friendly council.

I dont know that I told you that I had an idea of publishing a variety of Calotype subjects such as the omnia gatherum of the portfolio now with you. I have also an Idea that I would like to do Nuremberg [?] a work by itself. I have heard much of that ancient place and we have little of it yet in art . . .'[100]

Hill was clearly a little embarrassed by his over-enthusiasm in this letter and on 14 March wrote: 'I fear I displayed some bad taste in praising too much the works it adverted to, and perhaps in claiming more for my friends the Adamsons than Mr. Talbot or his friends would admit them to be entitled to. The Egotism you must forgive — and the praise of my friends is to *my friend* and to him only.' He referred again to his project of publishing: 'I still think perhaps a work of this sort would or might answer a sort of Liber Studiorum in its way. I have sometimes thought of calling it "A Book of 100 Calotypes".' He ended:

'I have spent some hundreds of pounds and a huge cantle [part] of my time in these Calotype freaks. I think the art may be nobly applied — much money could be made of it as a means of cheap likeness making — but this my soul loathes, and if I do not succeed in doing something by it worthy of being mentioned by Artists with honor — I will very likely soon have done with it. But I hope better things, for I do think that a truly noble work honorable to England — might in a few months be ready to go forth — and would earn more solid applause than the livid pictures of Daguerre'.[101]

Regrettably, much of what Hill and Adamson proposed in these letters came to nothing. Talbot did not respond within the next twelve months and they were unable to enter the English market as professional calotypists.

Hill was sufficiently interested in the technology of photography to join, early in 1845, the Royal Scottish Society of the Arts — an association devoted to the improvement of mechanics and crafts which had seen discussion of photography and the associated photographic processes (such as photomicrography and photolithography) since 1839. Robert Adamson was, curiously enough, not a member.

Hill was clearly making serious efforts to market the calotypes or at the least to encourage a favourable reception for them in 1845. One of his correspondents in London was Charles Heath Wilson, the Director of the Schools of Art at Somerset House who wrote to him in April: 'If I had had the calotypes I could have done a great deal. I have lately had important opportunities under very favourable circumstances, I have one friend especially who will prove an enormous puffer. I can send them to Mr. Rogers the Poet & to other people ½ doz. will answer the purpose perfectly. Mrs. Jamieson is going to take them up strong, but you should guide us what to say in case we get upon wrong ground in respect of the English patent.'[102]

Both Mrs. Jameson and Samuel Rogers were influential critics but it is not known if they did review the calotypes. The weightiest and most rabidly enthusiastic of the reviews proves to have been written by Lady Eastlake (then Miss Elizabeth Rigby) who had greatly enjoyed posing for Hill and Adamson at Rock House (Catalogue 114). Her review is planted arbitrarily in the middle of a review of books on modern German painting published in the *Quarterly Review* in 1846:

'One standard, however, there does exist, and one from which there is no appeal, for it rests upon demonstration, and not upon opinion. This is to be found in that wonderful source recently discovered — the only sure test for those artists who, professing to reflect Nature in their works, can by Nature herself only be judged. We mean the beautiful and wonderful Calotype drawings — so precious in every real artist's sight, not only for their own matchless truth of Nature, but as the triumphant proof of all to be most revered as truth in art. Every painter, high or low, to whom Nature has ever revealed herself, here finds his justification. Let Mr. Hill apply the Calotype instrument to a simple manly head in a commanding position, it creates a Sir Joshua, — give it an old face wrinkled with age, it returns us a Rembrandt, — summon three or four barelegged urchins, we see Murillo's beggar boys, — place it before a group of Newhaven fishermen, we have Tenier's Dutch Boors, or Ostade's Village Alehouse — or against a crumbling brick wall, and Peter Le Hooghe lies mezzotinted before us. Take it to tangled Sylvan landscapes, it presents us with a Hobbima, a Gainsborough, or even, what we had not sufficiently prized before, a Constable — give it fretted spires and leafy banks, distant towns and glittering streams, playful shadows and struggling lights, sunny storms and watery beams — and give it lastly, the very motes dancing in the air before them all — and the detractors of Turner lick the dust — the loftiest eulogy of Mr. Ruskin is justified. Every truth that art and genius has yet succeeded in seizing here finds its prototype; but what shall we conjure up in heaven or earth that shall produce a Düsseldorf picture? Nature disowns it.'[103]

Hill was apparently ill with rheumatism for part of the Summer and much of the Autumn of 1845 but reported to Roberts in December, 'I have never yet heard from Mr. Talbot — some fine things in his art have been produced by us since you last saw what we have done. Mr. Lockhart who was here lately — thinks with you that I should come to London in the Spring and I have heard from him since urging that measure — we will see.'[104]

In January, Hill was still talking of trying to effect an arrangement with Talbot and it may be that Lady Eastlake's review was a direct result of his increasing frustration. The Eastlake review was quoted by Hill's friend Dr. John Brown in *The Witness* in April 1846 where he said, amongst other things, 'in nothing has Mr. Hill shown his true love for, and his power over, the best part of his art, than in what he has accomplished in this department.'[105] These reviews were directed at Talbot himself as much as at the public. Lady Eastlake added to her article a footnote: 'To Mr. Fox Talbot the happy invention is owing, but that artistic application of it, which has brought these drawings to their present picturesque perfection, required the eye of an artist, and for this the public is indebted to Mr. D. O. Hill of Edinburgh, in conjuction with Mr. Adamson, a young chemist of distinguished ability. It is to be hoped that Mr. Talbot, in justice to his own genius, will soon invite these gentlemen to London — where they would find rather more interesting, though certainly not more grotesque subjects, than the fat Martyrs of the Free Kirk — as yet seemingly their favorite subjects.' (John Brown, writing for the Free Church newspaper quoted only the first half of the last sentence, thereby saving Hill some embarrassment.)

John Murray, the publisher of the *Quarterly Review* and a friend both of Hill and of Talbot wrote a tempered version of this to Talbot in May: 'I cannot refrain from wishing that it were possible for Mr. Hill to act in conjunction with you. There are points in which your Calotypes have the decided superiority over his — there are others in which I think he excels — especially in obtaining artistic effects — a combination of the two would be a step in advance.'[106] Talbot did not respond.

The year 1846 was remarkable for being warm and sunny. Adamson was able to take photographs at Rock House in January and the strawberries were ripening near Edinburgh early in February. In May, Hill and Adamson were involved in what may be the first attempt to bury photographs for posterity when seven calotype views were deposited in the foundation stone of the Free Church monument to John Knox in the High Street. This took place during the session of the Free Church Assembly and Hill took the opportunity to advertise again for sitters for the Disruption Picture. The newspaper report following this advertisement said that Hill had originally planned to take only three years to paint the picture: 'We understand, however, that a longer period must elapse before its completion, a circumstance which the doubling of the scale of the picture, and the insertion of twice or three times the number of portraits more than were at first contemplated, are sufficient to apologise for.'[107]

Hill had also undertaken another big picture, a view of Edinburgh from the Castle which was the reason for another of their more remarkable groups of photographs, of the 92nd Gordon Highlanders.

After 7 June 1846, which is the date of one of the more successful photographs of D. O. Hill and Dr. George Bell, there is a sudden stop in the flow of the dated negatives. Although less than ten per cent of the calotypes are dated, there is a strong implication that something went wrong in the studio at this point. It is very likely that Robert Adamson was already suffering from the illness which finally killed him in 1848. Hill first mentions this in a letter to David Roberts in August 1847 when he says, 'Adamson has been so poorly for many months that our calotyping operations have gone on but slowly . . .'[108]

The main output of the Rock House studio, some three thousand images, was therefore taken within three years — in real terms, a still shorter period, allowing for the inactive winter months. This is a phenomenally high number for an awkward process which requires bright light for taking and printing the photographs. When there is added to this the fact that both of the partners were seriously unwell at times and that Hill, as Secretary of the Academy, was closely involved from 1844 in an unattractive and lengthy dispute between the Academy and the Board of Manufactures who owned the building which housed the Academy exhibitions, it is hard to understand how they achieved it.

One group of photographs which may be dated to 1847 relates to another large painting, of the railway viaduct at Ballochmyle (Fig 17). The viaduct was only completed in March 1848 and Hill was painting there in August 1848, so it is conceivable that Hill tried to take these calotype studies after Adamson's death with Miss Mann or another assistant. However, the negatives are apparently numbered in Robert Adamson's hand. This particular photographic session was technically a complete failure, including the only double exposure produced by the partnership. The negatives are a peculiar muddy grey or purple colour and the few prints from them were clearly only made for Hill (some have paint or linseed oil smears on the back) for reference purposes.

A more successful photographic session which also may date to 1847 was a group of portraits taken for Lord and Lady Ruthven. Hill sent prints of these to Lady Ruthven in December 1847: 'Lady Haddo's and Miss Baillie's are not what in better circumstances we could hope — and so I may say of your own and Lord Ruthven's portraits — yet yours especially, indicates what could be done in this direction, with good sitters, good backgrounds and good sunshine: indeed with these appliances a wonderful little family gallery might be made in a few days and to such uses I do not doubt the Calotype will come'. The letter ends: 'I am preparing a calotype volume of 100 calotypes which I hope soon to show your ladyship. With its publication, the art and I will probably part company'.[109]

Lady Ruthven was an influential figure in the art world and a woman of both wit and character. The two known 'portraits' of her are both back views, possibly at her own insistence. It is a curious and sad coincidence that one of the last of the calotypes should be of a figure turning her back on the camera. By the time Hill wrote to Lady Ruthven, Robert Adamson had retired to St. Andrews. Early in 1848, he died there.

At Robert Adamson's death, Hill was left in a melancholy position. He wrote an apologetic letter to Samuel Carter Hall, the editor of the *Art Journal* who wanted to publish some of the calotypes, in August 1848:

'Your former note I got just as I was setting off to paint in the country where I remained some time, and as a settlement of my Calotype affairs was then pending between me and the friends of my late friend and partner [illegible] Mr. Robert Adamson, I put off writing to you, thinking then a very short period would enable me to write you definitively on the subject of your letter — either as the *sole* proprietor of the Calotypes — or as having given up any interest in them altogether. Still this matter is unsettled — and I arrived in Edinburgh only an hour ago . . . having come a distance of 100 miles solely to get this Calotype affair of ours arranged, but not meeting Mr. Adamson's brother as I expected *here,* I fear I will have to return to the country tomorrow without my errand having been accomplished.

I trouble you with all this in order to explain to you that I — not being the sole proprietor of the Calotypes, cannot say what I would wish to say — namely that you are welcome to make use of them for the Art Union Journal — and therefore I must speak for Mr. Adamson's relations who with myself have been put to heavy expenses by these our Calotype interests. I would propose that you pay [illegible] sum as you think the Journal can afford for the use of them — say if you please 25 guineas for 10 . . .'[110]

Hill's letter to Samuel Hall implies a tension and possibly even a quarrel between him and the Adamson family. The situation was apparently resolved with Hill keeping the calotype negatives and positives in stock —

17 *THE BRAES AND BRIDGE OF*
BALLOCHMYLE
BY DAVID OCTAVIUS HILL
OIL PAINTING
Reproduced by courtesy of Sir Claud
Hagart-Alexander, Bart

18 DAVID OCTAVIUS HILL
BY JOHN ADAMSON
ALBUMEN PRINT
Reproduced by courtesy of the Royal Museum
of Scotland

ROBERT ADAMSON AND DAVID OCTAVIUS HILL 43

possibly making some payment to the Adamsons. Dr. John Adamson encouraged Thomas Rodger to take up photography where Robert Adamson had left it — though in St. Andrews rather than Edinburgh — and it is evident that Hill had no intention of continuing with photography himself. Reasonably enough John Adamson seems to have taken Robert Adamson's standard-size camera at least back to St. Andrews, since both he and Thomas Rodger were using a camera of this size within the next few years.

The connection between Hill and the Adamson family did not cease with Robert's death. There are a number of photographs of Hill and his daughter taken by John Adamson in the 1850s and 1860s (Fig 18), which suggest that they visited St. Andrews and that Hill was taking a continuing interest in photography and may have been advising Thomas Rodger. The photographic portraits produced by John Adamson and Thomas Rodger are notably influenced by the Hill and Adamson calotypes of the 1840s, showing a sense of scale and solidity of composition. John Adamson, almost as silent a man as his brother, reacted forcibly against the prevailing taste for miniature photographs in the 1860s, in terms that are a clear echo of Hill: 'I wish very much that the large heads should be exhibited to advantage as I entertain a hope that they may in some small degree help to turn the public taste from the small "carte de visite" pictures so fashionable at present and in which I think the photographic art has been progressing *backwards* — to portraits of a larger size — and a more ambitious aim in the direction of the painter's field of operation'.[111]

Hill never recouped the considerable outlay he made on the calotype process. The volumes he had bound turned one by one into splendid gifts — to Clarkson Stanfield, to Lady Eastlake, to the Royal Academy — and he gave away hundreds of individual calotypes to Sir David Brewster, David Roberts and Henry Bicknell. Sales of the calotypes are mentioned only in small quantities. Hill was undoubtedly seriously depressed in January 1852 when the Great Exhibition had preferred the technical advances of photography at the expense of the calotypes: 'I had some hope the Chrystal Palace Fine Arts Jury would have awarded me a medal for my artistic application of this process — and I am still of the opinion they should have done so — it would have been some consolation for much time and money spent, I hope not foolishly, in making the art respectable.'[112]

At the end of the year Hill made his most splendid gift yet, to the Royal Scottish Academy. He wrote again to David Roberts about 'A project of mine to form a Calotype department of the Library of which I have formed the basis with 500 of my own. I think I have influence enough with not a few of the Calotypists to get copies of their best. These we propose to preserve in beautiful [?] volumes. Look one day to see this an important feature of our collection.'[113] Hill's attempt to form the basis of a valuable study collection of photographs as an art form received initial approval and enthusiasm from the Academy and from photographers in the 1850s. The remaining core of the collection, which he himself had given to the Academy, was ultimately destroyed in 1975 when the albums of calotypes were sold and broken up.

SCIENCE, PAINTING AND PHOTOGRAPHY IN SCOTLAND

It is a remarkable fact that right at the very start of practical photography, this revolutionary art form was so well understood that the earliest photographers were capable of exploiting it so thoroughly. It is characteristic of both Talbot's work and of Hill and Adamson's that they explored and experimented with the possibilities of the calotype process, scientific, practical and artistic, to its limits. This is partly because the invention of photography provoked not just surprise but also recognition.

Scotland in particular at the beginning of the nineteenth century held a pre-eminence in the dissemination of scientific knowledge. The English universities, under the strict and straitened control of the Church of England, were stifling rather than encouraging the advance of science. Many Englishmen who wished for a proper scientific education travelled either abroad or up to Scotland.

In Scotland at this time there was also an interchange between the artists and the scientists — a coincidence of interests and an attractive social connection between them, and a kind of over-the-fence curiosity and exchange of ideas. Two of the leading figures in the intermixed worlds of science and art were to have a strong influence on both D. O. Hill and Robert Adamson: Sir David Brewster and Alexander Nasmyth.

Sir David Brewster was a vigorous, bright-eyed, argumentative character: 'In the walk, at the meal, in society, in solitude, there was a constant observing and experimenting upon some common daily occurence — the colours and forms of plants, the eye balls of fish and other creatures, the habits of gold-fish, the gambols of mice, abounding in his old house, the scratching of snail shells on the window, the jewels and tinted ribbons of his lady visitors, the patterns of wallpapers and carpets, the shadows of carriage blinds . . .' One of Brewster's friends, 'himself the possessor of genial gifts and genius', remarked to his daughter, 'When I have been with other great men, I go away saying, "What clever fellows they are"; but when I am with Sir David Brewster, I say, "What a clever fellow I am".'[114] This clearly was Brewster's attractive side and is certain evidence that he was stimulating and interesting company. His drive and enthusiasm had its opposite effect in overbearing wrong-headedness. Sir David Brewster was not one to accept a contrary view, and his company must often have been as irritating as it was stimulating.

His close association with painters had led him to no great respect for their ability to think: 'Poets and painters have, generally speaking, very imperfect conceptions of the force of mathematical and physical evidence. The predominance of the imagination over the judgement indisposes them for patient and profound thought.'[115] This opinion comes in Brewster's review of Goethe's *Theory of Colours* as translated by Charles Lock Eastlake. Brewster's own erroneous theory of colours depended on a three-colour system, red, yellow and blue, whereas Goethe favoured a seven-colour spectrum. Eastlake, examining Goethe's spectrum, concluded that the harmonious opposite of scarlet was a pearly grey. Brewster's theory demanded that the harmonious opposite of scarlet should be bright green — that is, a mixture of the two other primaries. Brewster pursued his belief in such 'harmony' into the art exhibitions. William Salter Herrick recalled that he 'often deplored the want of scientific knowledge in the whole English school. He seemed to me to regard the few pictures that show real harmony of colour in each Exhibition rather as the result of a feeling for colour than the result of knowledge. He would take an instrument from his pocket, about two inches long, with two holes in it, which allowed of shifting glasses to show the complementary colours, by which he would demonstrate that, even when a picture appeared to be true in colour, the disproportion of the hues of the reds and yellows, with their complementaries, showed how much further a little real knowledge of the principles would have carried the artist.'[116] Brewster went further than mere criticism and offered practical advice: 'We conceive, however, that some assistance, and that not inconsiderable, might be derived from direct experiments, in which a painter himself should judge of the relative effects of different colours, when placed in juxtaposition. In order to do this, we must combine *colours* with *form,* and the only ready way of effecting this is to place the actual colours on the palette, and reflect them into symmetrical forms by the kaleidoscope.' With the best will in the world it is impossible to picture the Scottish painters poised over palettes splotched with the primary colours, kaleidoscope in hand, deriving any practical benefit from the idea.

Brewster was in this instance not so much crossing boundaries as trespassing on the painters' territory. Nevertheless, there he was. His constant stirring presence in the art field made him at the very least, a catalyst. More important, he was a man who thought everything his province, and nothing was impossible.

Under Brewster's influence, Mrs. Talbot observed that the reticent, unsociable Talbot broke into sociability. Brewster was responsible for persuading Talbot to allow the calotype process to be practised in Scotland and he acted as the spokesman for the St. Andrews calotypists in their long-drawn-out trials and failures. His persistence and the determination showed by Major Playfair and Dr. John Adamson are the reasons the calotype process ever succeeded, and it was at Brewster's suggestion that Robert Adamson became a professional photographer. It was also Brewster who sought out D. O. Hill and persuaded him to meet Robert Adamson, and he maintained an interest in their work, carrying examples about with him and recommending Adamson to prospective clients.

Sir David Brewster was a frequent visitor to the house of the landscape painter, Alexander Nasmyth. Forty-seven York Place, the Nasmyth house, is described in the autobiography of his son James Nasmyth, in lyrical terms:

'When the day's work was over, friends looked in to have a fireside crack — sometimes scientific men, sometimes artists, often both. They were all made welcome. There was no formality about their visits . . . Among the most agreeable visitors were Professor Leslie, James Jardine, C.E., and Dr. Brewster. Their conversation was specially interesting. They brought up the last new thing in science, in discovery, in history, or in campaigning, for the war was then raging throughout Europe.

The artists were a most welcome addition to the family group. Many a time did they set the table in a roar with their quaint and droll delineations of character. These unostentatious gatherings of friends about our fireside were a delightful social institution. The remembrance of them lights up my recollection of the happiest period of a generally happy life.'[117]

At parties of this kind and in long walks round Arthur's Seat and out into the country, Alexander Nasmyth and his friends discussed every current subject from geology to town planning, with a small James Nasmyth pattering along behind, all ears. Alexander Nasmyth was a man of wide-ranging ability, not just painting landscapes but making them, designing bridges, inventing methods for walking on water or coming quickly down steep hills (Fig 19). He had the kind of quirky, constructive intelligence that responded to a query by the Duke of Atholl as to how to plant trees in a bare inaccessible crag, by filling a cannon with tree seeds and firing at it. Astonishingly, the trees grew. He and his

19 'METHOD OF DESCENDING VERY STEEP MOUNTAINS WITH EASE AND SAFETY' BY ALEXANDER NASMYTH, 1812 CHALK DRAWING
Reproduced by courtesy of the National Gallery of Scotland

wife were of an amiable temperament — prepared to let their son use his bedroom grate as a working forge — and created an atmosphere in which ideas and art flourished side by side. It is no coincidence that Mary Somerville, later the distinguished mathematician, who was sent to Nasmyth's painting classes to learn a genteel ladylike occupation which would not strain her mind too far, first learnt about Euclid's *Geometry* in his house.

D. O. Hill was a pupil of Alexander Nasmyth and of *his* pupil, Andrew Wilson. Hill spent much time in York Place and James Nasmyth remained a close friend throughout his life.

The link between these social groups and photography comes in theoretical terms in the insistence of both scientists and artists on the need to look to nature for truth rather than simply to follow the example of the great masters of the past. Imitation without understanding led to mistakes and to mannerisms. The practical connection which gave them a mutual interest lay in the subject of light.

The technology of photography was already partly to hand, in the camera obscura. The Nasmyth household not only used cameras but could make them with no difficulty (Fig 20). The camera lucida, which is not truly a camera but a similar aid to drawing which drove Talbot to invent photography, induced ideas of 'photographic truth' before photography was invented. A close friend of Alexander Nasmyth, James Hall of Dunglass, commissioned his brother, Basil, to do a series of camera drawings: '. . . having conceived the novel and bold idea of representing Sir Walter [Scott] exactly as he appeared in company, without any of the contrivances by which other painters have studiously concealed the defect of his right foot, he begged me to secure some careful jottings with the camera for this purpose. I told Sir Walter the reason why I wished to sketch him leg and all; at which he laughed repeatedly, and said his young friend's idea was not a bad one.'[118] The fact that Basil Hall's drawings are dire in the extreme, and that James Hall's painting which used them is even worse, did not shake their conviction that this experiment in truth was worth while.[119]

A more successful 'pre-photographic' exercise in drawing with light took place over the road from the Nasmyth house in York Place. The landscape painter and diarist, Joseph Farington, visited Sir Henry Raeburn's Edinburgh studio in 1801 and inspected his work: 'Some of Mr. Raeburn's portraits have an uncommonly true appearance of Nature and are painted with much firmness, — but there is great inequality in his works. — That which strikes the eye is a kind of Camera Obscura effect, and from those pictures which seem to be his best, I shd. conclude He has looked very much at Nature, reflected in the Camera.'[120]

Raeburn's painting is distinguished by a powerful interest in light. His portraits were expressed in terms of the way the light blocked out a sitter rather than in terms of the figure's outline (Fig 21). He achieved this in his York Place studio by turning the whole room into something like a camera, turning the concept upside down by putting his sitters *in* the camera rather than outside it. The north-facing studio has one enormous window which not merely reaches the ceiling but is cut into it. The external stonework above is cut in at an angle to allow yet more light to enter. On either side and at the top of the window, an elaborate system of small shutters could be closed or opened to allow greater or less light to enter. He was thus able, in modern photographic terms, to increase or decrease the aperture of his light source and to control the level and quality of light within the room.

Clearly enough, the landscape painters like Alexander Nasmyth

view from the drawing room
window of my House at
Patricroft nr Manchester

Drawn in a camera obscura
made in 15 minutes – by me
June 13. 1841 James Nasmyth

The camera obscura was rigged up out of an old Tin Box
with a spectacle Eye as the Lens to explain to my wife the construction of a camera

21 WILLIAM FORBES OF CALLENDAR
BY SIR HENRY RAEBURN
OIL PAINTING
Private collection, on loan to the Scottish
National Portrait Gallery

20 'VIEW FROM THE DRAWING ROOM
WINDOW OF MY HOUSE AT
PATRICROFT NR MANCHESTER. DRAWN
IN A CAMERA OBSCURA MADE IN 15
MINUTES BY ME JUNE 13 1841 JAMES
NASMYTH. THE CAMERA OBSCURA WAS
RIGGED UP OUT OF AN OLD TIN BOX
WITH A SPECTACLE EYE AS THE LENS TO
EXPLAIN TO MY WIFE THE
CONSTRUCTION OF THE CAMERA'.
BY JAMES NASMYTH
INK DRAWING
Reproduced by courtesy of the National Library
of Scotland

and D. O. Hill could not import whole landscapes into the controlled conditions of a studio, although Nasmyth did make little trees for his pupils to study. But the nineteenth century brought a developing interest in landscape seen in terms of light and space rather than physical outline. The interest in transient light effects presented a simple practical difficulty — how to catch the effect before it faded. The landscape painters had to develop an intense way of seeing to imprint the memory of these effects — a kind of personal photography — linked to an understanding of the effects which would enable them to recall them successfully. Painters like John Constable and J. M. W. Turner had this skill; painters like D. O. Hill were trying to achieve it and occasionally succeeded.

The note on Hill's death published by the *Scotsman* on 17 May 1870 says, 'His style of landscape belonged rather to the poetic than to the naturalistic school, and many of his pictures show him to have been a warm admirer, and indeed imitator of Turner.' This is undoubtedly true. Turner was associated with the Edinburgh painters primarily through John Thomson of Duddingston who shared with him the work of illustrating Walter Scott's *Provincial Antiquities of Scotland.* The active influence of the Scottish circle on Turner appears in his painting after every visit. His first tour in 1801 saw him sketching with a new freedom and rapidity which marked the break with the traditional topographical painting of his youth. He was influenced in later years by David Brewster's theories of colour and light, and must have been one of the few painters who tried out Brewster's idea of the necessary harmony of red, blue and yellow.[121]

Hill's painting technique echoes Turner's in, for instance, his use of edged lines of paint for highlights. But the resemblance goes deeper. In 1847, Hill's close friend, Dr. John Brown, wrote an enthusiastic critical review of John Ruskin's *Modern Painters.* He said of the work that 'it asserts and proves the existence of a new element in landscape painting, placing its prince [i.e. Turner] on his rightful throne.' The new element involved several ideas — that landscape painting was more than a mechanically correct picture of the solid shape of the land; that it required 'aerial perspective' (the light and colours of distance); that it required an eye guided by intelligence, so that an intelligent sketch could be preferred to a polished painting and, more seriously, that a thoughtful failure should be rated above a mindless success. John Brown completed his review by considering three pictures in Ruskin's terms. The three were one of Turner's own sketches in his *Liber Studiorum,* George Harvey's *Glen of the Enterkin,* and a sketch by Hill taken from his window in Inverleith Row. Hill's sketch was 'done in a fine frenzy of an hour; it has exquisite colour, and is as sweet and deep in its tones as his own voice; but what is it? Look and you will see, wait and you will feel. There is nothing of earth to be seen but the tops of some great trees, among them an old fir with its cones of last year. Lying across them, and giving them power, and getting for itself distance and freedom, is a long line of evening sky: under it and above it clouds of unimaginable colours. The broad sun is sinking, all but sunk down "in his tranquility" and in that line of light, added by the painter (for though the sea was not visible to his eye, he wanted it to be there) you see the sea! and on it is the gentleness of the upper heavens. There we have a scene in itself imaginative to all minds of ordinary sensibility, made more so by a mind of higher sensibility, which works under an exalted condition of its whole nature. And fixes for ever upon that mere sketch, the strong and delicate but evanescent feeling as well as sensations of that hour.'[122]

Hill had himself urged John Brown to take up art criticism for *The Witness* newspaper in 1846 and Brown had agreed because 'I was anxious to do it very much on account of David Hill. I want to tell the truth about him to himself and the public.'[123] Brown's ideas were evidently close to Hill's. As early as March 1845, Hill had expressed his enthusiasm for *Modern Painters* in a letter to David Roberts, which said he was 'fascinated with the truth and beauty of his [Ruskin's] remarks'.[124]

Hill expressed direct admiration of Turner in 1850, when requesting the loan of his *Wreck of a Transport Ship* from Lord Yarborough — the painting most admired by Ruskin in *Modern Painters* — for the 1851 Royal Scottish Academy exhibition: 'Nothing I am sure could better show to this portion of the island, the greatness of the mind and the giant power of the poet-painter of the ocean, than this most noble work; indeed I feel that its presence among us would give new aspirations, and higher resolves to our whole school'.[125] As additional points of connection, Hill owned a portrait sketch of Turner by Sir William Allan and Turner's published work the *Liber Studiorum*.

In the calotype of the publisher, John Blackie, Hill's own main published work, *The Land of Burns* (with Hill's name carefully written in on the spine in the calotype negative), leans comfortably against the *Liber Studiorum* (Fig 22). This work, a series of engravings of Turner's landscapes, was not just a piece of self-advertisement on Turner's behalf. It had an educational, academic purpose, to classify and illustrate the different kinds of landscape as a visual demonstration of his theories of painting. It is of notable importance that when Hill talked to David Roberts about selling bound volumes of the calotypes, he referred to his plan as 'a sort of Liber Studiorum in its way'. This meant that Hill thought of the calotypes in the same experimental, educational light — and Hill's 'Liber Studiorum' was nine-tenths figure studies, an extension of Turner's idea, not an imitation of one volume of landscapes by another.

22 JOHN BLACKIE
BY D. O. HILL AND ROBERT ADAMSON
CALOTYPE
Scottish National Portrait Gallery

LIGHT AND DETAIL IN THE CALOTYPE

this is backwards!

The subtle light effects of the calotype were made possible partly by the process itself. The calotype is 'printed out', that is to say the negative remains in contact with the positive for the whole of the printing process — a process which could take up to two hours depending on the quality of the negative. The great advantage of this was that detail in the dark areas could be developed without bleaching out the light areas. Bright sunshine, which would achieve a harsh contrast in modern processes, could result in a more diffused effect in the calotype. The city of Edinburgh itself may have added to this diffusion. To the south of Calton Hill lay the Old Town of Edinburgh, known as 'Auld Reekie' from the quantities of smoke rising from thousands of coal fires (Fig 23). Sunlight filtering through the wavering coal gases would have turned into a dispersed light of great photographic subtlety.

Hill and Adamson's calotypes show a practical interest in varied lighting. Thomas Davidson's concave mirror (described above) was used outside the camera as a reflecting light source, and it can be seen in certain of the photographs that they used weaker light reflections from unpainted canvasses (Fig 24), light drapes, papers and books. These light sources are visible in the photographs when there is a logical reason for them to be there, and it can be assumed that they were using a greater range of light reflectors 'off-camera'.

Their enthusiasm for the calotype as a method of creating a lively 'painting in light' is the reason Hill rarely took a landscape photograph. Two practical problems made it difficult and the results unsatisfactory. Firstly, green was a colour to which the photographic chemicals were insensitive, and trees in leaf were apt to photograph as unattractive dark masses. Secondly, it was impossible to photograph the ground and the sky together; an exposure time long enough to take the darker land would result in a blank white, or oddly mottled, sky. In his painting Hill was devoted to the rich, luminous effects of sunsets and twilights and the subtleties of distant graduated light which were Turner's 'aerial perspective'. This was impossible with the calotype and Hill's pleasure in the process recognised its limitations. The most powerful of their photographs are taken in a comparatively shallow focal range which exploited the lack of detail rather than showing it up as a failing.

Since it is often implied that Hill was a bad painter who took up photography as an easy way out of his problems, it is worth emphasising this point. What he did with photography bore little relation to his painting; with the calotype he was seizing the opportunity to do something new.

D. O. Hill's enthusiasm for the calotype is distinguished from that of Talbot or Brewster or from that of other professional calotypists. His comparison of the calotype with the daguerreotype reads: 'The rough and unequal texture throughout the paper is the main cause of the calotype failing in details before the Daguerreotype . . . and this is the very life of it. They look like the imperfect work of man and not the much diminished perfect work of God.'[126] On an earlier occasion he hoped that his own work with the calotype 'would earn more solid applause than the livid pictures of Daguerre.'[127]

Hill regarded the calotype specifically as an art medium and rejected the daguerreotype *because* it was more detailed and more truthful — a belittling of nature rather than an interpretation. The strong character and limitations of the calotype were interesting in themselves — the little, precise, shiny daguerreotype concealed nothing and said nothing. Robert Adamson consistently worked to a richly-coloured coarse standard in which the contrast between the light and dark stayed strong and massed rather than precisely drawn.

Talbot and Brewster thought of the calotype as an improvable

23 DETAIL FROM *EDINBURGH OLD AND NEW*, SHOWING THE VIEW SOUTH FROM THE CASTLE WITH THE QUANTITIES OF SMOKE PRODUCED BY THE EDINBURGH HOUSES.
BY D. O. HILL
OIL PAINTING
National Gallery of Scotland

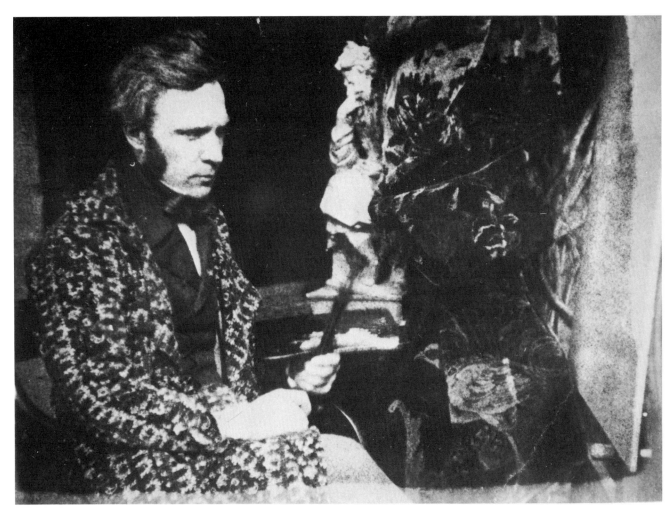

24 SIR GEORGE HARVEY
BY D. O. HILL AND ROBERT ADAMSON
CALOTYPE
Scottish National Portrait Gallery

process, lacking in detail and precision. Talbot's discussion of his photograph, 'The Haystack' in *The Pencil of Nature* talked of the calotype as though it were a daguerreotype: 'One advantage of the discovery of the Photographic Art will be, that it will enable us to introduce into our pictures a multitude of minute details which add to the truth and reality of the representation but which no artist would take the trouble to copy faithfully from nature' (Catalogue 93).

Brewster, who knew Hill and Adamson's calotype portraits well, and indeed was given large numbers of them, remained of the opinion that the calotype was unsuitable for portraiture. He reviewed the progress of photography in 1847 and said of calotype portraits:

'The defect is so great, as to deter many persons from sitting for their portraits; for when other defects arising from the unsteadiness of the sitter, and the painful expression, which arises from exposure to strong light, are added to the picture, it is often a hideous likeness, even when female beauty has submitted to its martyrdom. The defect arises, to a certain extent, from the rough grain, so to speak, of the paper, and also from its imperfect transparency — for in the positive picture every imperfection of the paper is copied, and every luminous point re-appears as a black one — so that the positive picture has the appearance of being stippled, as it were, with grains of sand, which give a painful coarseness to the human face.'

Brewster continued the review by recommending his own improvement of the calotype which involved oiling or varnishing the negative, exposing the untreated side of the paper in the camera for two or three times the usual time, and then varnishing or oiling the positive which gave an image 'greatly softened'. He added to these oily, softened pictures the dismal possibility that they could be 'improved, or rather varied in their character, by placing coloured paper behind them'.[128]

Professional calotypists like Henry Collen and Claudet improved the calotype by painting on top: 'Likenesses are now produced upon paper, which are then placed before a competent artist who "touches them up", and makes of them PORTRAITS . . . wrought upon by an accomplished miniature painter, Mr. Mansion.'[129] Here again, it is interesting that Hill, whose painting was characterised as poetic, that is to say involving a manipulation of the truth towards the ideal rather than the literal, resisted the temptation to decorate the calotypes. The Hill and Adamson calotypes are remarkable for the restrained touching up of the negatives. Except in rare cases (Catalogue 114), they only removed evidence of supports and chemical faults and occasionally strengthened the lines of drapery or hair.

Brewster's article quoted above must have seriously shaken Hill and Adamson. His wholesale condemnation of calotype portraits appeared in the *North British Review* — an influential academic journal. It must have been in response to this that Hill persuaded Lord Cockburn to ask the editor of the *Edinburgh Review* if he would publish 'an article on Art — chiefly Calotype' by Dr. John Brown. Lord Cockburn added: 'This application proceeds from certain artists here — who hold that this is the Paradise of Calotype — an opinion on which they are supported, I believe, by Landseer, Stanfield, Eastlake & other competent judges; & no doubt (but this is only my suspicion) they want their own glorification, — incorporated into a general article.'[130] The article did not appear, possibly because the editor responded to the note of warning in Cockburn's letter, but many judges then and now would readily agree that Scotland *was* the 'Paradise of Calotype'.

NOTES

68. Fox Talbot Museum, ms. 43-53 letter Sir David Brewster to Talbot, 9 May 1843.

69. *British Journal of Photography,* 22 August 1879: p.400.

70. James Good Tunny, 'Early Reminiscences of Photography', *British Journal of Photography,* 12 November 1869, p.545. A later version of this story, with Thomas Davidson throwing the sash weight, appeared in 1879: see previous note.

71. *Journal of Henry Lord Cockburn 1831-1854,* vol. II, p.26.

72. Quoted in *Disruption Worthies. A Memorial of 1843,* 1876, p.xvi.

73. Quoted in the prospectus for the photographs by Thomas Annan of the finished picture, *An Historical Picture Representing the Signing of the Deed of Demission painted by D. O. Hill, RSA,* no author but presumably by D. O. Hill, 1866, p.4.

74. Science Museum, ms. letter Brewster to Talbot, 3 July 1843.

75. Advertisement in *The Witness,* 8 July 1843.

76. Hugh Miller, 'The Calotype', *The Witness,* 12 July 1843.

77. James Good Tunny, op. cit.

78. Dr. C. G. Carus, trans. S. C. Davison, *The King of Saxony's Journey Through England and Scotland in the year 1844,* 1846, p.337.

79. Royal Observatory, ms. letter James Nasmyth to D. O. Hill, 30 April 1845.

80. Royal Observatory, ms. letter Nasmyth to D. O. Hill, 27 March 1847.

81. Private collection, ms. letter D. O. Hill to David Roberts, 12 March 1845.

82. Royal Scottish Academy, ms. letter D. O. Hill to C. G. H. Kinnear, 14 December 1856.

83. Thomas Davidson, letter to the Editor, *Liverpool Photographic Journal,* October 1859, p.264. Davidson had made a mirror camera for himself by 1841, which he described in a paper read at a meeting of the Royal Scottish Society of Arts on 11 January 1841 (National Library of Scotland, ms. Acc. 4534/107).

84. Ibid.

85. Science Museum, ms. letters Brewster to Talbot, 18 and 28 November 1843.

86. Quoted in Daphne Foskett, *John Harden of Brathay Hall 1772-1847,* 1974, p.52.

87. Royal Scottish Academy, ms. letter Sir Thomas Dick Lauder (Secretary to the Board) to Hill and Adamson, 22 December 1843.

88. Science Museum, ms. letter Brewster to Talbot, 18 April 1844.

89. *Edinburgh Evening Courant,* 3 August 1844.

90. Private collection, ms. letter Hill to David Roberts, 26 April 1845.

91. Reported in the *Fife Herald and Kinross, Strathearn and Clackmannan Advertiser,* 25 January 1844.

92. Advertised and reported in the *Liverpool Mercury,* 6 September 1844.

93. Fox Talbot Museum, ms. 44-67 letter Hill to Talbot, 21 September 1844.

94. *Journals and correspondence of Lady Eastlake,* ed. Charles Eastlake Smith, 1895, p.151, 19 December 1844.

95. Royal Observatory, ms. letter James Nasmyth to Hill, 30 April 1845.

96. *Edinburgh Evening Courant,* 29 October 1844.

97. Royal Scottish Academy, ms. letter David Roberts to Hill, 9 November 1849.

98. Private collection, ms. letter Hill to Roberts, 25 February 1845.

99. Private collection, ms. letter Hill to Roberts, 14 March 1845.

100. Private collection, ms. letter Hill to Roberts, 12 March 1845.

101. Private collection, ms. letter Hill to Roberts, 14 March 1845.

102. Royal Scottish Academy, ms. letter Charles Heath Wilson to Hill, April 1845.

103. Review of books on modern German painting (untitled), *Quarterly Review,* March 1846, pp.337-8.

104. Private collection, ms. letter Hill to Roberts, 19 December 1845.

105. Dr. John Brown, review of the Royal Scottish Academy exhibition, *The Witness,* 22 April 1846.

106. Fox Talbot Museum, ms. letter John Murray to Talbot, 19 May 1846.

107. *The Witness,* 28 May 1846.

108. Ms. letter Hill to Roberts, 12 August 1847, present whereabouts unknown.

109. Royal Scottish Academy, draft ms. letter from Hill to Lady Ruthven, December 1847.

110. Edinburgh Public Library, ms. letter from Hill to Samuel Carter Hall, 21 August 1848.

111. Scottish Record Office, GD 356/12/71 ms. letter from John Adamson to the Photographic Society of Scotland, 29 November 1861.

112. National Library of Scotland, ms. Acc. 7723, Hill to David Roberts, 14 January 1852.

113. National Library of Scotland, ms. Acc. 7723, Hill to David Roberts, 18 November 1852.

114. Mrs. Gordon, *The Home Life of Sir David Brewster,* 1869, p.302 and p.299.

115. Sir David Brewster, review of Goethe's *Theory of Colours,* translated by C. L. Eastlake, *Edinburgh Review,* October 1840, p.124.

116. Mrs. Gordon, op. cit., 3rd edition 1881, pp.147-8.

117. *James Nasmyth, Engineer, An autobiography,* ed. Samuel Smiles, 1883, p.52.

118. Captain Basil Hall, *Fragments of Voyages and Travels,* 3rd series new edition, 1852, p.167.

119. The drawings and the painting are now in the Scottish National Portrait Gallery, ref PG 2656 to PG 2662 and PG 937. See Helen Smailes, 'Sir Walter Scott in Camera', *The Bulletin of the Scottish Society for the History of Photography,* Spring 1986, pp.2-5.

120. *The Diary of Joseph Farington,* ed. Kenneth Garlick and Angus MacIntyre, vol V, 1979, p.1631, 23 September 1801.

121. See John Gage, *Colour in Turner. Poetry and Truth,* 1969, p.126.

122. Dr. John Brown, review of volumes 1 and 2 of *Modern Painters, North British Review,* 1847, vol 6, pp.401ff.

123. *Letters of Dr. John Brown,* ed. by his son and D. W. Forrest, 1907, p.64.

124. Private collection, ms. letter D. O. Hill to David Roberts, 12 March 1845.

125. John Paul Getty Museum, ms. accession 84 × G 1003 letter from Hill to David Roberts, 10 January 1850. I am indebted to Graham Smith for drawing my attention to this letter.

126. Letter from D. O. Hill to Elhanan Bicknell, 17 January 1848, quoted in Colin Ford and Roy Strong, *An Early Victorian Album. The Photographic Masterpieces (1843-1847) of David Octavius Hill and Robert Adamson,* 1976, p.30.

127. Private collection, ms. letter Hill to David Roberts, 14 March 1845.

128. Sir David Brewster, review of the progress of photography, *North British Review,* vol 7, 1847, p.479.

129. *The Art Union,* June 1845, p.171.

130. National Library of Scotland, ms. Dep. 235 letter Lord Cockburn to William Empson, 22 November 1847.

PLATE 1
3   CLIMBING PLANT IMPRESSION

PLATE 2
14 MAN IN THE CLOISTERS, LACOCK
    ABBEY

PLATE 3
16 BEECHWOOD IN SUNLIGHT

PLATE 4
40   HONEYSUCKLE

PLATE 5
50   WINDSOR, ST JAMES CHAPEL

PLATE 6
73 MAN WITH A CRUTCH

PLATE 7
76   THE CHESS PLAYERS

PLATE 8
78 HUNGERFORD SUSPENSION BRIDGE,
    OPENED IN 1845

PLATE 9
122 PRINCES STREET WITH THE SCOTT
     MONUMENT, 1845

PLATE 10
131 JAMES DRUMMOND

PLATE 11
139   MARY McCANDLISH

PLATE 12
146   UNKNOWN WOMAN

PLATE 13
151   AT THE MINNOW POOL

PLATE 14
168   MRS. ELIZABETH HALL AND ANOTHER
       FISHWIFE

PLATE 15
191   TREE AT COLINTON

PLATE 16
195 92ND GORDON HIGHLANDERS AT
        EDINBURGH CASTLE

WILLIAM HENRY FOX TALBOT

CATALOGUE

In his earliest photographic publication of January 1839, Talbot explained how he made his first photographic images: 'I proposed to spread on a sheet of paper a sufficient quantity of nitrate of silver, and then to set the paper in the sunshine, having first placed before it some object casting a well defined shadow . . . The first kind of objects which I attempted to copy by this process were flowers and leaves, either fresh or selected from my herbarium. These it renders with the utmost truth and fidelity, exhibiting even the venation of the leaves, the minute hairs that clothe the plant, etc.'[1]

The paper goes on to describe the feature of photography which was to impress and enchant Talbot in all his photographic work: 'It is so natural to associate the idea of labour with great complexity that one is more struck at seeing the thousand florets of an Agrostis depicted with all its capillary branchlets . . . than one is by the picture of the large and simple leaf of an oak or a chestnut. But in truth the difficulty is in both cases the same. The one of these takes no more time to execute than the other; for the object which would take the most skillful artist days or weeks of labour to trace or to copy, is effected by the boundless powers of natural chemistry in the space of a few seconds.'[2]

During 1839 Talbot made a great number of flower and leaf prints. When these were shown to the public and the details of the process became known, many others shared Talbot's enthusiasm and marvelled at the precision of the images and the detail captured. According to *The Mirror*, 'Objects the most minute are obtained, — the delicate hairs on the leaves of plants, — the most minute and tiny bivalve calyx, — nay even a shadow, the emblem of all that is most fleeting in this world, is fettered by the spell of the

FLOWER AND LEAF PRINTS

SEE COLOUR PLATE 1
3 CLIMBING PLANT IMPRESSION

1 LEAF IMPRESSION (NEGATIVE)

4 COMPOUND LEAF IMPRESSION
(POSITIVE)

2 PRUNUS LEAF IMPRESSIONS (NEGATIVE)

invention, and remains perfect and permanent long after it has been given back to the sunbeam which produced it.'[3]

Most of the early experimenters soon transferred their interest to camera pictures but a minority recognised and exploited the potential of Talbot's first process. One of the earliest to do so was Dr. Golding Bird who wrote in *The Magazine of Natural History,* 'I feel that the application of this heliographic or photogenic art will be of immense service to the botanist, by enabling him to procure beautiful outline drawings of many plants, with a degree of accuracy which otherwise he could not hope to obtain.'[4] Using Herschel's cyanotype (blueprint) process, Anna Atkins practised the same technique to produce a privately printed and published part-book, *British Algae: Cyanotype Impressions,* between October 1843 and 1853. This has been described as the first serious application of photography to scientific publication.[5] Talbot himself was still sufficiently interested in leaf printing to reproduce a specimen in *The Pencil of Nature* in 1844 and the accompanying text suggests he was planning to publish further specimens at a later date.[6]

1. H. F. Talbot 'Some Account of the Art of Photogenic Drawing', *Philosophical Magazine XIV,* 1839.
2. Ibid.
3. *The Mirror.*
4. Golding Bird, 'Observations on the application of Heliographic or Photogenic Drawing to Botanical Purposes' *The Magazine of Natural History,* Vol. 3, 1839, pp. 188 - 192.
5. See Larry J. Schaaf, *Sun Gardens, Victorian Photograms by Anna Atkins, 1855, 19866. H. Fox Talbot, The Pencil of Nature,* 1844, notes to Plate VII.

LACE

In 1839 Talbot's pictures, prepared by simply placing lace or fabrics on sheets of sensitive paper and exposing them to light, charmed and fascinated all who saw them. The reaction of the highest in the land as reported to Talbot by Lady Theresa Digby was typical: 'Many thanks for the drawings which I showed to the Queen yesterday . . . they met with universal admiration . . . I am sorry to tell you that the Queen was more struck by the exactness of the ribbon than the beauty of the ferns and grapes . . . the gauze ribbon she said was very curious and she must try to do some herself'.[1] Talbot's mother was prompted to suggest a few days later, 'I understand the Queen being no botanist admired most the ribbon you sent her. Therefore I have in mind to send you a bit of beautiful point lace which I think would have great success — shall I?'[2] Even the scientist, David Brewster, who could be relied on to appreciate the simplicity of the operation necessary to produce them, thought the lace pictures 'especially' interesting. In the light of this popularity, it is not surprising that Talbot chose to include no less than ten photogenic drawings of lace (and two magnified views made with the solar microscope) in the first major public exhibition of his work at the British Association meeting at Birmingham in August 1839. Some five years later when Talbot had considerably improved his process, he used a lace negative to explain the principles of his negative/positive technique in *The Pencil of Nature*. Here, he made the point that in the case of lace 'a negative image is perfectly allowable, black lace being as familiar to the eye as white lace, and the object being only to exhibit the pattern with accuracy'.[3]

1. Fox Talbot Museum, ms. letter Lady Theresa Digby to Talbot, 13 April 1839.
2. Fox Talbot Museum, ms. letter Lady Elisabeth to Talbot, 18 April 1839.
3. H. Fox Talbot, *The Pencil of Nature,* notes to Plate XX.

5 LACE

6 LACE

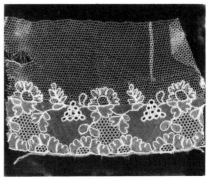

7 LACE (NEGATIVE)

PHOTOMICROGRAPHS

Talbot's accounts of his early work suggests that the first pictures he produced with the aid of an optical instrument were made not with a camera obscura but with a solar microscope. As he recorded later, 'I succeeded in my attempts, chiefly in consequence of a careful arrangement of the Solar Microscope, by which I was enabled to obtain a very luminous image, and to maintain it steadily on the paper during five or ten minutes, the time requisite.' The images captured seemed to Talbot to be 'curious and wonderful as they are often singularly complicated. The eye, indeed, may comprehend the whole which is presented to it in the field of view, but the powers of the pencil fail to express these minutiae of nature in their innumerable details. What artist could have skill or patience enough to copy them?'

Talbot seems to have made a considerable number of photomicrographs in 1839, a great many of which he gave away to friends such as Sir John Herschel and Sir Walter Calverly Trevelyan. However, as Talbot explained, 'After the invention of the calotype process, it became of course a comparatively easy matter to obtain these images, and I then ceased to occupy myself with this branch of photography, in order to direct my whole attention to the improvement of the views taken with the camera.'[1]

1. *Journal of The Society of Arts,* No. 25, 13 May 1853, p.191.

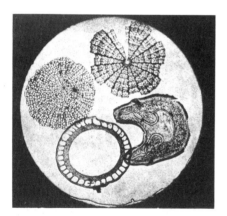

8 DIATOMS

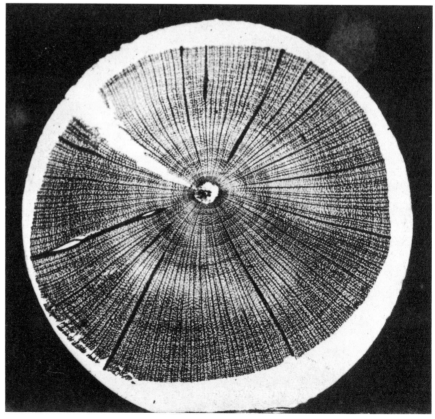

9 TRANSVERSE SECTION STEM (NEGATIVE AND POSITIVE)

Talbot's first photographs with a camera were of his country home, Lacock Abbey. In his Royal Society paper of 1839, he claimed the house as, 'the first that was ever yet known to have drawn its own picture'[1] and repeated this claim later in *The Pencil of Nature*. Talbot was in fact wrong in his belief but if Lacock Abbey was not the first house to be photographed, for a time it must have been the house that was most photographed.[2] It was certainly the subject Talbot photographed most often as he recorded it again and again from every angle and viewpoint. In the first major exhibition of his photographs in August 1839 Talbot showed 93 photogenic drawings. Just twenty of these images were made with the camera and all of them were views of, or taken from, Lacock Abbey.[3]

In a sense, all of these early views were experimental and indeed the Abbey was Talbot's ideal test subject. He knew it intimately in every light and every weather; it was always unvarying and always convenient. But later Talbot made many studies of the Abbey which are fine photographs and were highly praised by contemporary critics. Reviewing Plate XIX of *The Pencil of Nature*, 'The Tower of Lacock Abbey', the author in *The Literary Gazette* recorded:

'These genuine sun-pictures (Apollo's own workmanship) seem almost to improve in accuracy and effect, as if the Solar Artist, like a human hand, had become more master of his powers by practice and experience. The tower of

LACOCK ABBEY

10 LACOCK ABBEY IN WILTSHIRE (*THE PENCIL OF NATURE*, PLATE 15)

Lacock Abbey is a rich and picturesque subject; upon which the distribution of light and shadow is curiously natural, and very striking as a truth, if we might say so, beyond the conceptions of imitation. It is difficult to explain this — it consists in the faintest gradations of light throughout, not only the broader masses, but the most minute parts of the picture, and sinking into a darkness almost complete, but nevertheless not black. It must be carefully examined to have this remarkable quality fully understood and appreciated.'[4]

1. H. F. Talbot, 'Some Account of the Art of Photogenic Drawing,' *Philosophical Magazine XIV,* 1839, p.206.
2. The earliest surviving photographic image was taken in France by Nicéphore Niépce in 1826. It was a view of part of his house at Chalon.
3. H. F. Talbot, 'A Brief Description of the Photogenic Drawings Exhibited at meetings of the British Association at Birmingham, August 1839'. A printed list in the Science Museum, Fox Talbot Collection.
4. *The Literary Gazette,* No. 1512, 10 January 1846, p.38.

SEE COLOUR PLATE 2
14 MAN IN THE CLOISTERS, LACOCK ABBEY

11 THE CLOISTERS OF LACOCK ABBEY (*THE PENCIL OF NATURE,* PLATE 16)

12 THE TOWER OF LACOCK ABBEY (*THE PENCIL OF NATURE,* PLATE 19)

see note below ↑↓

13 TWO MEN IN THE COURTYARD, LACOCK ABBEY

15 MAN AT THE DOORWAY, LACOCK ABBEY (SMALL PRINT)

which of these two images (11 & 15) is reversed?

In 1841 one of the most influential of Talbot's photographic contemporaries wrote: 'I have been recently favoured with a communication from Mr. Talbot accompanied by some most exquisite specimens of this new photographic art. One of these drawings, an elm tree, was effected by an exposure of one minute in the camera, and the minutest details, even "the topmost twigs that look up at the sky" are given with considerable strength and much picturesque effect.'[1] The writer was Robert Hunt, author of the first major photographic instruction book, commentating on some early calotypes. Like all early photographers he was very well aware of the skill and patience required to draw a finely detailed object such as a tree and intrigued by how easily and quickly it could be recorded by the camera. Talbot delighted in recording intricate details, and very early in his experiments he must have discovered that trees made fine photographic subjects for he made a great number of tree images using both the photogenic drawing and calotype processes.

TREES

1. Robert Hunt, *A Popular Treatise on the Art of Photography,* 1841.

SEE COLOUR PLATE 3
16 BEECHWOOD IN SUNLIGHT

17 TREES AND REFLECTIONS

19 TREES IN WINTER (NEGATIVE)

18 ELM IN WINTER

ARTEFACTS AND SPECIMENS

Talbot's interest in recording small artefacts either singly or as a collection is yet another manifestation of his delight at the ease and subtlety with which the camera could record detail and also his preoccupation with light and the manner in which it was reflected from different surfaces and textures.

Talbot published two characteristic calotypes in *The Pencil of Nature* entitled 'Articles of China' and 'Articles of Glass'. The contemporary reviews of these images clearly show that Talbot was not alone in his interests. *The Literary Gazette* noted: 'The third plate is of four rows of articles in china. They are all exceedingly curious. A boy and a china basin with a bird upon it, on the right of the centre vase in the second row, are the most perfect facsimiles of the articles they copy that we ever saw, and yet either might be drawn on the space of a thumb-nail. The next is glass — decanters, tumblers, carafes, wine glasses, etc. — in three rows: and the reflected lights being the most remarkable portion of the spectacle.'[1] *The Athenaeum's* comment was: 'The minute details exhibited in the two plates displaying porcelain ornaments and glass are exceedingly curious and beautiful, and they improve under examination with a powerful lens.'[2]

Neither commentator remarked upon Talbot's propensity to see photography as a working tool when he noted how quick it was to photograph the specimens in comparison to the usual chore (for the time) of preparing a written inventory. Nor did they comment on his futuristic suggestion: 'And should a thief afterwards purloin the treasures — if the mute testimony of the picture were to be produced against him in court — it would certainly be evidence of a novel kind'.[3]

1. *The Literary Gazette*, No. 1432, 29 June 1844, p.410.
2. *The Athenaeum*, No. 904, 22 February 1845.
3. H. Fox Talbot, *The Pencil of Nature*, 1844, notes to Plate III.

21   BOOKS ON SHELVES

22   PORCELAIN ON SHELVES

24   CANDELABRA

23   BONNETS (THE MILLINER'S WINDOW)

25   TEAPOT, SUGAR BOWL AND CANDLE
      (NEGATIVE)

STILL LIFE STUDIES

Talbot made a number of pictures using as subjects various utilitarian objects which would have been conveniently to hand in the grounds of Lacock Abbey. A reviewer in *The Literary Gazette* of 1840 writes of 'old walls and buildings with implements of husbandry; of carriages; of tables covered with breakfast things'.[1] Talbot sent examples of work in this style to his friend Herschel later the same year where they clearly found favour. In his letter of thanks Herschel wrote: 'I am very much obliged indeed by your very very beautiful photographs. It is quite delightful to see the art grow under your hands in this way. Had you suddenly a twelvemonth ago been shown them, how you would have jumped and clapped hands (i.e. if you ever do such a thing).

That which pleases me most is I think (for it is difficult to choose) the garden scene with trees and trellis. It is very unlike any drawing . . . Then the corner of a sunny wall with garden tools — How admirably the broom shows — and the shine of the spade'.[2]

A number of these views are undoubtedly further examples of Talbot imitating the Dutch painters in the style of 'The Open Door' which Talbot published in *The Pencil of Nature*. The objects are arranged in what Talbot thought was a pleasing way, perhaps to stimulate those 'picturesque imaginings'. Other items are simply photographed as they stand, probably because Talbot thought they had curious shapes or reflections and would make interesting studies in line and form and the distributions of light and shade. Yet again, others reflect his long term fascination with the ability of the camera to record detail and subtleties of texture.

There is no evidence to suggest that Talbot thought any more of these photographs than that they were interesting experiments in picture construction. They do not form a large proportion of his total output. He also seems to have produced most of them rather early in his photographic career and probably over a limited period.

26 BROOM AND SPADE BEFORE FOLIAGE

Few examples of this style of work appear on any of the various surviving lists of photographs which were later printed for sale. It may be that Talbot experimented with this form of still life subject whilst he was forced to use long exposures and his options were limited. As soon as he had perfected his calotype process he moved on to, what were for him, more interesting studies.

1. *The Literary Gazette,* No. 1217, 16 May 1840, p.315.
2. Science Museum, ms. letter Herschel to Talbot, 19 June 1840.

28   CART AND LADDER

27   CARRIAGE AND LADDER

THE ROCKING HORSE

According to his granddaughter, the rocking horse shown was presented to Talbot for his children about 1840. He was called Firefast, we are told, because he was said to gallop so fast that he struck fire from the stones in the road. Firefast still survives in excellent condition and is normally displayed at Lacock Abbey.[1]

Talbot seems to have taken a considerable number of views of the rocking horse and the suspicion must be that he used it as a test subject in the same way that he used Patroclus. From what is known of Talbot it is also easy to imagine that he was persuaded to use it by the children.

1. According to Matilda Talbot, *My Life and Lacock Abbey,* 1956.

29 THE ROCKING HORSE

In his first photographic paper of 1839, Talbot stated: 'Another use which I propose to make of my invention is for the copying of statues and bas-reliefs . . . I have not pursued this branch of the subjects to any extent; but I expect interesting results from it'.[1] The original idea was undoubtedly to present to artists and those interested in art a more accurate and truthful representation of sculpture and statuary on paper than had ever been possible before. Talbot had every reason to expect this application of his invention to be popular for at the time of writing interest in the reproduction and multiplication of works of art was a fashionable preoccupation and part of the wider 19th-century interest in the effects of industrialization on culture. Talbot's instincts were probably correct and a wide selection of calotypes of busts, statues, bas-reliefs and figurines were certainly printed for sale. *The Art Union,* with a prophetic glimpse into photography's future, saw this branch of Talbot's art as a useful aid to the architect and modeller: 'The Talbotype would at least ensure fidelity of detail without any sacrifice of the general character of the design . . . It is rarely that the copies taken by artists of architectural or other monuments contain sufficient information for the working modeller . . . we scarcely know any instance of a good copy of an ornament being reproduced by a sketch . . . We believe that Talbotypes would be found in many instances preferable to casts; but at all events they could be obtained where casts are unobtainable, as in copying parts of edifices and in the tracery of minute architectural details.'[2]

Talbot must have very quickly found that static subjects with interestingly variable surfaces such as sculpture made excellent subjects for his photographic experiments. It is evident that he became quite intrigued by aspects of photography that had not previously occurred to him, as he records in *The Pencil of Nature*: 'These delineations are susceptible of an almost unlimited variety: since in the first place, a statue may be placed in any position with regard to the sun, either directly opposite to it or at any angle: the directness or

SCULPTURE AND STATUARY

30 PATROCLUS

obliquity of the illumination causing of course an immense difference in the effect. And when a choice has been made of the direction in which the sun's rays shall fall, the statue may then be turned round on its pedestal, which produces a second set of variations no less considerable than the first.'[3]

The subject reproduced in *The Pencil of Nature* is a bust of Patroclus. Talbot was, evidently, so taken by it that he reproduced a different view in a later issue. Talbot's enthusiasm was shared by his contemporaries. Of the earlier reproduction *The Literary Gazette* wrote that it was 'really sublime in style and effect'[4] and of the later, 'A bust of Patroclus displays great force and illustrates in another way, or at least another kind of subject the truthfulness of the Royal road to drawing for which we are so deeply indebted to Mr. Talbot.'[5]

It is difficult for the modern eye, conditioned by exposure to a million pictorial images, to appreciate fully this enthusiasm. Yet the more innocent eye of the 19th century was undoubtedly excited by the realism of these representations which in this particular case would have been enhanced by the coarse grained structure of the calotype print.

1. H. F. Talbot, 'Some Account of the Art of Photogenic Drawing,' *Philosophical Magazine XIV,* 1839, p.206.
2. *The Art Union,* 1 July 1846, p.195.
3. H. Fox Talbot, *The Pencil of Nature,* 1844, notes to Plate V.
4. *The Literary Gazette,* No. 1432, 29 June 1844, p.410.
5. *The Literary Gazette,* No.1488, 26 July 1845, p.500.

31 AN ARRANGEMENT OF SCULPTURE
    WITH THE THREE GRACES IN CENTRE

32 FOUR SETS OF SCULPTURE ON A SINGLE
    SHEET (VARNISHED CALOTYPE)

Talbot saw the production of photographic copies of engravings, manuscripts and the like as one of the most valuable features of his invention. His attitude reflected a wider public interest in the reproduction of works of art which Talbot undoubtedly hoped to exploit commercially. *The Art Union's* remarks were typical of the comment of the period when it noted that Talbot's process had a 'most valuable capability — that of increasing ancient manuscripts and valuable drawings upon the material whereon they were originally made, and so fitting them for the portfolio.' It went on to record perceptively, 'The powers of the Talbotype are admirably adapted to book illustrations.'

      Talbot also emphasised the value of producing facsimiles of documents and manuscripts and thus anticipated photocopying. His experiments with the production of documents in reduced sizes are the first step on the road towards modern microfilm techniques.

COPIES OF ENGRAVINGS, BOOKS AND MANUSCRIPTS

34   COPY OF ENGRAVING OF A SHELL

33   COPY OF ENGRAVING

35   COPY, BOTANICAL ENGRAVING 'CELTIS'

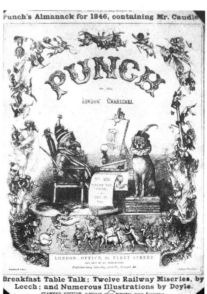

37   COPY, REDUCED SIZE, TITLE PAGE OF *PUNCH* NO. 233, 27 DECEMBER 1845 (NEGATIVE AND PRINT)

36   COPY, ENGRAVING OF JOHANNES JACOBUS SCHEUCHZERUS BY NUTTING

CAMERA PICTURES OF FLOWERS AND FOLIAGE

It seems likely that Talbot's interest in botany and horticulture would have led him into attempts to make camera pictures of flowers and shrubs at an early date. However, this was not as straightforward as it might have seemed. It is well known that modern photographic emulsions do not 'see' colours in the same way as the human eye, that is, they are not uniformly affected by the visible spectrum. This characteristic was even more marked in the early processes which were rather insensitive to objects coloured green. The problem was outlined in *The Athenaeum*:

'There is another physical difficulty under which all the photographic processes alike suffer. These pictures are formed by the chemically active rays which are reflected from the illuminated object, and these rays vary in quantity considerably with the colour of the reflected body. If we place side by side, in the sunshine, objects coloured blue, green, yellow and red, and attempt to copy them by the camera with any photographic material, it will be found that the blue will make the most decided impression — the green will be much weaker, the red also will give a faint impression, but the yellow will scarcely leave an impression of its image. This in practice will often be found to give exaggerated effects to the chemical picture; and the imperfect manner in which foliage, under the most favourable conditions is represented, is attributable to the radiations from the surfaces of leaves being very deficient of the chemically active rays.'[1]

This characteristic was recognised by the French scientist, Biot, who when seeing an early calotype of Talbot's reported that the ivy appeared too dark because of the insensitivity of the salts to green rays,[2] and by Herschel who remarked on 'the difficulty of doing foliage at all'.[3]

To produce a representation of a flowering plant or shrub in any context would therefore have presented Talbot with some uncomfortable problems, for the long exposures necessary to give a reasonable impression of green foliage would almost certainly mean that much of the rest of the picture

was over-exposed. This problem explains the dense, sombre backgrounds of many of Talbot's outdoor views where green foliage of one sort or another forms the backdrop.

1. *The Athenaeum,* No. 904, 22 February 1845, p.202.
2. In a letter from Biot to Talbot of March 1841. Quoted by D. B. Thomas, *The First Negatives,* 1964.
3. Science Museum, ms. letter Herschel to Talbot, 19 June 1840.

SEE COLOUR PLATE 4
40 HONEYSUCKLE

39 FLOWERS ON A CHECK TABLECLOTH

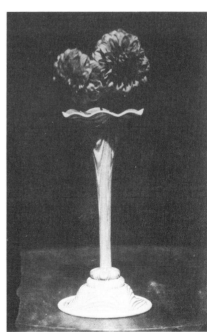

42 TWO FLOWERS IN VASE

41 GNARLED TREE

COUNTRY HOUSES
AND ESTATES

Talbot took many photographs at the country houses and estates of his family and friends. Talbot and his camera must have been a popular and unusual diversion for visitors to the great country houses and it might be suspected that for many of them he was part of the summer entertainment.

Mount Edgecumbe in Devon, the country seat of Lord Valletort, the husband of Talbot's half-sister Caroline, seems to have been a particularly favoured summer sojourn for the Talbot family. In September 1844 Caroline wrote to Talbot imploring him to join the party: 'I wish you would think better of it and come and see us at the same time as Mamma and Lord Aukland (*sic*) — I think you would find it a pleasant party and one that would suit you, as you know the Bonnevals and all of them so well. I should think you might manage to make Calotypes even in Company, if you brought one of your own people to help you. Particularly in our Italian climate, you wd. have fewer obstacles than you generally meet with'.[1] A year later, after an 1845 visit, Constance his wife wrote: 'I do long to see the Mount Edgecumbe views, particularly the battery scenes'.[2] This would suggest that Talbot made only negatives on his trips away from home and the prints were made at Lacock or the Reading Establishment.

An indication that views taken at the country houses were popular and might even be marketable can be found in a draft prospectus drawn up, probably by Talbot and Henneman together, around 1847. Headed by the title, 'By Royal Letters Patent, Sun Pictures or The Talbotype', it lists a series of subjects for which calotype photography was particularly suited. Prominently sited in the document is the offer, 'Noblemen and Gentlemen may have any number of different views taken of their Seats, ornamental Buildings, Etc., and each view multiplied indefinitely.'[3]

1. Fox Talbot Museum, ms. LA 44-57 letter Lady Caroline to Talbot, 7 September 1844.
2. Fox Talbot Museum, ms. LA 45-136 letter Constance to Talbot, 12 October 1845.
3. A printed sheet with many hand-written amendments and revisions. Science Museum, Fox Talbot Collection.

43 MOUNT EDGECUMBE

44   VIEW FROM MOUNT EDGECUMBE

45   ETON HALL, GATEWAY

TOWNS AND BUILDINGS

By 1841 Talbot had improved his technique to the point where he was eager to extend the scope of his photographic activities. In March of that year he wrote to Herschel: 'I must now transport my apparatus to some locality where picturesque objects are to be met with, such as a Cathedral, or a Seaport Town, for my own neighbourhood is not particularly suited to the artist, and offers no great variety of subjects.'[1]

During the subsequent five years Talbot took his camera to towns and villages up and down the country, sometimes alone but often with a helper or companion. Amongst the places he visited were Oxford, Cambridge, Windsor, York, Bristol, Brighton, Chester and Stratford.

He returned several times to Oxford and the pleasure he must have derived from his photographic expeditions is reflected in a letter to his mother written in September 1843: 'When you left me at Steventon I procured a conveyance but got out at Abingdon and walked from thence to Oxford in the cool of the evening — part of the way lies through a pretty forest — the distance is seven miles. The weather has been exceedingly fine both Monday, Tuesday and today and I have made about twenty views each day, some of which are very pretty — but the number of picturesque points of view seems almost inexhaustible.'[2]

He also visited York on more than one occasion with both Henneman and also the Rev. Calvert Jones. It was in the company of the latter in July 1845, that he wrote: 'We took 12 views . . . today . . . most of them good — crowds of admiring spectators surrounded the camera wherever we planted it'.[3]

Talbot's architectural photography was a branch of his work which was admired almost without reservation in the 1840s, and his example was quickly followed. The popular attitude of the period can be summed up by an extract from *The Art Union* in 1848: 'When it is remembered that Photography enables us to copy, in a few seconds, the most extensive architectural pile, with all the details of elaborate tracery and highly ornamental

46   CURVE OF OXFORD HIGH STREET

48   GONVILLE AND CAIVS COLLEGE, CAMBRIDGE

47   ORIEL COLLEGE, OXFORD

columns . . . when, in addition, Photography is found to furnish the best studies of perspective and preserve graduations of light and shadow in their natural beauty and consistency, it will require no argument to convince our readers of the real value of this beautiful art.'[4]

1. Quoted by H. J. P. Arnold, *William Henry Fox Talbot,* 1977, p.95.
2. Fox Talbot Museum, ms. LA 43-76 letter Talbot to Lady Elisabeth Feilding, 6 September 1843.
3. Quoted by Arnold, op.cit. p.145.
4. *The Art Union,* 1 May 1848, p.133.

SEE COLOUR PLATE 5
50 WINDSOR, ST JAMES CHAPEL

49 YORK, STREET WITH MINSTER IN BACKGROUND

TALBOT'S FAMILY

Members of Talbot's family and his closest friends were the subjects of his earliest calotypes. Yet, despite the experimental nature of so many of these photographs, Talbot was rewarded with what are surely amongst the most successful of his portraits.

Talbot saw a great deal of his family, especially his mother, his half sisters, Horatia and Caroline, and of course his wife, Constance, and his children. Talbot had three daughters, Ela, born in 1835, Rosamund, born in 1837, and Matilda, born in 1839. His only son, Charles Henry, was born in 1842.

Talbot has been portrayed by some historians as a severe, rather cold man but this is not borne out by the surviving correspondence which shows him as a much loved figure at the centre of a warm, affectionate family. This picture is certainly borne out by his only granddaughter: 'Though I had seen him only once, in that long ago summer of 1877, I remembered his kind face and his kind voice ... I believe we children thought of him as something almost supernatural. My mother (Matilda) so often told us how much he knew about the stars, their names, how far off they were and so on. Then she constantly spoke of his interest in flowers — how many rare and distant things he obtained from distant places and made them grow at Lacock Abbey.' She went on to give a glimpse of Talbot the patient father of young daughters: 'His three little girls used to play at battledore and shuttlecock in the Great Hall, and its walls echoed with their shouts and laughter. But he would never tell them to stop — he just came along the passage and shut the intervening doors.'[1]

The portraits of Talbot's daughters are particularly charming and must reflect the relaxed, happy relationship he enjoyed with his family. The images almost look like snapshots of half a century or so later yet they would have required careful posing. Children can, of course, make splendid actors but one can imagine their carefully suppressed excitement as they were coaxed into entering into the spirit of father's game.

1. Matilda Talbot, *My Life and Lacock Abbey,* 1956.

51   ELA WITH FLOWER

52   ROSAMOND '17 AUG 1843'

53   MATILDA LEANING ON STOOL

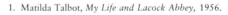

56   CAROLINE AND HORATIA

54   THE THREE DAUGHTERS AT LACOCK

57   CAROLINE AND HORATIA IN THE
     CLOISTERS

55   HORATIA WITH HARP

CONSTANCE TALBOT

Talbot married Constance at All Souls, Langham Place in London on 20 December 1832. Constance was twenty-one at the time and Talbot described her as having 'the disposition of an angel'.[1] Many years later his young granddaughter painted a rather different picture: 'I was not so much drawn to my grandmother; she looked very severe. Perhaps she felt that we were not sufficiently disciplined. Meals at Lacock Abbey were rather solemn . . . there was no pleasing the woman whatever one said.'[2] But perhaps Victorian grandmothers could be expected to be stern with young granddaughters and in 1877, when this encounter took place, Constance was an elderly lady. Back in 1832 when Talbot's mother heard of her son's intended marriage she wrote: 'If you have found a person who will understand the value of your mind, I must love her, because she will certainly not be a common character.'[3]

The evidence suggests that Constance was indeed far from being a common character. Her support and encouragement for her husband's work can almost be taken for granted but her involvement with photography was far greater and more direct than is commonly realised. Indirectly, of course, it dates from the very beginning, for it was on his delayed honeymoon that Talbot first conceived the idea of a photographic process. Later, Constance did a great deal of printing for Talbot as the correspondence makes clear. On 23 March 1841, she wrote to him: 'As soon as the weather cleared I made two copies of the little picture — the first fifteen minutes, the second thirty minutes but in neither case did the sun shine through without interruption.' On 13 June the same year, Talbot wrote from London: 'Pray send me two or three copies of enclosed portrait. If the fixing liquid is exhausted send them wrapped and I will fix them here.' Again, Constance wrote to Talbot: 'I have made these three pictures myself and Porter has fixed them'.[4]

Other correspondence suggests that Constance probably also took photographs of her own. Sadly, it has so far proved impossible to identify specific images taken or processed by perhaps the first lady photographer.

58   CONSTANCE WITH HER DAUGHTERS
(NEGATIVE AND MODERN COPY PRINT)

1. Quoted by H. J. P. Arnold, *William Henry Fox Talbot,* 1977,p.62.
2. Matilda Talbot, *My Life and Lacock Abbey,* 1956, p.18.
3. Quoted by Arnold, op.cit., p.61.
4. All correspondence here quoted by J. Dudley Johnston, O.B.E. (ed. R. C. Smith), 'William Henry Fox Talbot, F.R.S.', *Photographic Journal,* vol. 108, No. 12, December 1968. The original correspondence is in the Lacock Abbey Collection.

In September 1840, Talbot discovered that a brief exposure in the camera produced what we now call a latent image which could be developed to produce a visible image. This new process Talbot called the calotype process. As he explained, 'One of the most interesting applications of the new process, and most likely to prove the most important, is undoubtedly the taking of portraits. I made a trial of it last October, and found that the experiment readily succeeded. Half a minute appeared to be sufficient in sunshine, and four or five minutes when a person was seated in the shade, but in the open air. After a few portraits had been made, enough to shew that it could be done without difficulty, the

PORTRAITS

59 PORTRAIT OF A GENTLEMAN

60   GENTLEMAN READING A BOOK AT
LACOCK 'JULY 1842'

experiments were adjourned to a more favourable season.'[1] The earliest known portrait by Talbot is of his wife, Constance, dated 10 October 1840.[2]

Talbot produced a great number of portraits and clearly worked hard to produce satisfactory results. However, as always, he seems to have been more interested in perfecting his technique and refining his process than in producing broad artistic effects, a point made with varying degrees of realism by his critics.

In July 1841 Talbot's uncle, William Fox Strangways, commented, 'The portrait is wonderful — but why do you not take a more interesting one? Constance with the three babies on their donkey and the Tower of Lacock behind would make a pretty picture!'[3] Henry Collen, the first professional calotype portrait artist, wrote to Talbot in May 1842:

'I have to thank you for the specimens rec'd today, as well as some on a former occasion which I forgot in my haste to acknowledge. The armchair is very successful, but in several of the others, the tints are very far from clear and solid. This is uniformly the case with mine, and to make them otherwise costs me much labour and consequent expense. The light background which you have much recommended and make great use of, gives certainly a clear sharp outline, but not an artistic effect, — you also make your pictures almost always in sunshine, which is however not to be used when the public please to sit.'[4]

Later the same year Talbot's Welsh cousin 'Kit' Talbot wrote: 'I think you ought to experiment on backgrounds to your portraits. For instance a black absorbent background, such as velvet or plush. Again a perfectly white sheet, and then note the effect produced upon the portrait itself. I make these remarks because all the selections I have seen of yours, seem to me to be badly chosen and not to do justice to the subject.'[5]

1. *The Literary Gazette,* 13 February 1841, p.108
2. See Gail Buckland, *Fox Talbot and the Invention of Photography,* 1980. The calotype is in the collection of the Royal Photographic Society.
3. Fox Talbot Museum, ms. letter William Fox Strangways to Talbot, 2 July 1841.
4. Fox Talbot Museum, ms. LA 42-31 letter Henry Collen to Talbot, 12 May 1842.
5. Fox Talbot Museum, ms. LA 42-64 letter Christopher Rice Mansel Talbot to Talbot, 24 August 1842.

61   LADY IN A STRIPED DRESS

62   LADY CHARLOTTE TALBOT (WIFE OF C. R. M. TALBOT)

Talbot's comments in *The Pencil of Nature* would seem to indicate an enthusiasm for photographs of people posed in groups: 'Groups of figures take no longer time to obtain than single figures would require, since the camera depicts them all at once, however numerous they may be: but at present we cannot well succeed in this branch of art without some previous concern and arrangement.

But when a group of persons has been artistically arranged, and trained by a little practice to maintain an absolute immobility for a few seconds of a time, very delightful pictures are easily obtained. '[1]

Many of Talbot's most pleasing groups are apparently informal photographs of his family, friends and acquaintances taken at Lacock or in the grounds or surrounding countryside of other country houses. The poet, Thomas Moore, in his memoirs tells of an occasion he witnessed: 'August 18, 1841 . . . started for Lacock Abbey this morning on my way to town. The day beautiful and I found grouped upon the grass before the house Kit Talbot, Lady E. Feilding, Lady Charlotte and Mrs. Talbot for the purpose of being photogenised by Henry Talbot who was busily preparing his apparatus'.[2]

In contrast to Talbot's apparently casual family groups and portraits there are some much more obviously 'constructed' pictures which include people posed in attitudes of work or with utilitarian objects. They are perhaps imitations of the style of painting with which he was most sympathetic and most familiar. Talbot took a great number of groups and portraits but surprisingly few of these photographs depicting people seem to have been made available to a wide public. This may be because the majority of them included members of the family, servants, or friends and he regarded the photographs as personal and private. However, it seems as likely that he simply lacked confidence in his artistic taste and was wary of criticism, particularly of an area of his work which clearly looked towards conventional art and did not simply reproduce nature. There was reason for him to be cautious for there was no shortage of critics. His mother's judgement was, 'There is no doubt if you were

GROUPS AND FIGURE COMPOSITIONS

an artist instead of an amateur your art would soon be the summit of perfection.'[3] In the press, he would not have been encouraged by the comparisons made of his own work with that of some of his contemporaries. The comment by Robert Hunt in *The Art Union* is an example: 'Many of the productions by the patentee of the Calotype process — Mr. Fox Talbot — involving the use of the gallo nitrate of silver may be seen at his place of business in Regent Street: they are exceedingly beautiful, but inferior, on the whole, to the artistic photography of Messrs. Hill and Adamson, of Edinburgh or those of several members of the Photographic club.'[4] Talbot was probably objective enough to realise that Hunt's words had as much to do with the patent disputes as the quality of his photographs but he was a sensitive man and the criticism must have hurt.

1. H. Fox Talbot, *The Pencil of Nature,* 1845, notes to Plate 14, 'The Ladder'.
2. Quoted by D. B. Thomas, *The First Negatives,* 1964.
3. Fox Talbot Museum, ms. LA 44-60 letter Lady Elisabeth to Talbot, 13 September 1844.
4. *The Art Union,* June 1848, p.238.

64   THE FRUIT SELLERS

66   C. R. M. (KIT) TALBOT AT THE BOTANIC GARDEN, OXFORD

65   COUPLE IN THE CLOISTERS

69 MAN AT A PUMP WITH FLASKS

67 ELDERLY COUPLE IN A DOORWAY

70 SAWING AND CLEAVING

68 TWO LADIES IN THE CLOISTERS

72 THE HAND-SHAKE

71 MEN WITH A NET AND A BASKET

WORKING PEOPLE

The photographs of working people are particularly interesting although there is little to suggest that Talbot was making a special record or any social comment. However, the photographs were taken at a time when Britain was just emerging from a prolonged depression. For Wiltshire, this was only one part of a much longer period of persistent economic decline and there had been considerable social unrest in the county.[1] Talbot, as a member of the gentry, and a shy man, might have been expected to find relations with working people difficult. In fact, the evidence suggests that there was a mutual respect between Talbot and his tenants.[2] Certainly, these photographs could not have been taken without the willing co-operation of the subjects.

The photographs show yet again Talbot's interest in line and form and his fascination with detail. Unfortunately, most of these studies have only survived as negatives. They are not products of Talbot's early work and such positives as were made would probably have been printed at the Reading Establishment. That so few are in evidence today may suggest that they were not popular in the 1840s and comparatively few were produced.

1. See, for example, J. F. C. Harrison, *The Early Victorians 1832-51,* 1971 and E. P. Thompson, *The Making of the English Working Class,* rev. 1968 edition.
2. See H. J. P. Arnold, *William Henry Fox Talbot,* 1977 and Matilda Talbot, *My Life and Lacock Abbey,* 1956.

SEE COLOUR PLATE 6
73 MAN WITH A CRUTCH

74 THE GAMEKEEPER AGAINST A STONE BUTTRESS

75 MEN AND A LAD IN THE WOODYARD

CHESS PLAYERS

Talbot took several photographs of chess players, the most successful being these two studies taken in the studio of the daguerreotypist, Antoine Claudet, around 1844.

The posing of these photographs must have been the subject of much discussion between Talbot and Claudet but the influence of the latter is likely to have been very strong. He was a close friend of Talbot's and a fine portrait photographer himself. Claudet appears in both calotypes — he is the sitter without the hat.

These two studies are amongst the very few calotypes featuring people that Talbot was prepared to offer for sale to the public. There exists a printed list of calotypes in which Talbot has priced in his own hand the sum of '7/6' (37½p) for a copy of the Chess Players.[1] An indication of his view of their relative merits is that he priced various views of Lacock and York at '5/-' (25p) and '3/-' (15p). (According to one authority the average wage of an agricultural worker in Wiltshire during this period was around 7/- (35p) a week.)[2]

Although little specific information is available, it is not difficult to speculate why Talbot the scientist should have been attracted to what has been termed 'Science in play'. The subject is static (and therefore easily staged for photography) yet dramatic. Talbot's calotypes have recently been described as 'a study in concentration rather than a record of two people'.[3] Chess has been played in England at least since the 12th century and has been a constant stimulus to the imagination of the artist. Talbot is likely to have been familiar with this art, perhaps particularly the popular engravings of Cruikshank of the first quarter of the 19th century and the lithographs of John Doyle of 1837.

1. An uncatalogued printed list in the Lacock Abbey Collection. A similar more complete list but without Talbot's annotations exists in the Science Museum, Fox Talbot Collection.
2. See J. F. C. Harrison, *The Early Victorians 1832-51*, 1971.
3. 'Chess in Art & Society', a leaflet published to accompany the exhibition of the same name produced by the Department of Prints & Drawings and Photographs, Victoria & Albert Museum, February 1986.

SEE COLOUR PLATE 7
76 THE CHESS PLAYERS

77 THE CHESS PLAYERS (ALTERNATIVE VIEW)

TALBOT'S LONDON

Talbot had a London house in Sackville Street, Piccadilly, and it was from here between 1841 and 1845 that Talbot and his associates made the most important surviving early record of what was then the world's first city.[1]

The picture Talbot's calotypes present of London is in some ways unreal, for it depicts an eerie, empty city of massive buildings and broad streets peopled only by the occasional ghost-like figure. The streets were of course filled with bustle and life but appear empty because Talbot's comparatively long exposures failed to capture moving objects. The length of Talbot's exposures cannot have been helped by the peculiar nature of the London atmosphere which posed a problem he would not have encountered at Lacock. In the 1840s smoke from thousands of factory and domestic chimneys meant that the city air was rarely completely clear. Talbot was certainly in no doubt as to the persistent and pervasive nature of the London air, for the very first entry in his 1839 notebook reads: 'Copperplates for engraving, if kept in London become tarnished by sulphurous vapours . . .'[2] An 1846 reviewer of *The Pencil of Nature* remarks on 'a rich view of Westminster Abbey curiously affected by atmospheric tints.'[3]

In order to minimise the problems caused by London's atmospheric pollution, Talbot may have worked early in the day when the air was clearest — and the city least crowded which would explain the empty streets.[4]

1. Talbot's calotypes are the earliest substantial record of London but three daguerreotype views made by M. de St. Croix in 1839 have survived. Two are in the Collection of the Science Museum, London; the third has recently been purchased by the Victoria & Albert Museum.
2. London, 6 February, Talbot's 1839 Notebook 'P', Science Museum, Fox Talbot Collection.
3. *The Literary Gazette*, 9 May 1846, p.433.
4. For a comprehensive account of early photographs of London, see Gavin Stamp, *The Changing Metropolis*, 1984.

SEE COLOUR PLATE 8
78 HUNGERFORD SUSPENSION BRIDGE,
    OPENED IN 1845

81 LINCOLN'S INN, NEW HALL LIBRARY,
    c.1845

79 WHITEHALL, THE BOARD OF TRADE
    AND PRIVY COUNCIL OFFICE, 1845

80 SOMERSET HOUSE, THE RIVER FRONT
    AND ESPLANADE

The familiar monument to the British naval hero was first proposed in the year of his death, 1805, but the site was not finally decided until 1838. The competition for the construction of the column was won by William Railton. The monument, which is over 145 feet high, took three years to build between 1840 and 1843. It was on 3 November 1843 that the sixteen foot high statue of Nelson by E. H. Baily was finally placed in position. Shortly after this date Talbot took his best known calotype view of the base of the column, probably from an upstairs window in Cockspur Street. A later 1845 view from the same site shows work completed on the surrounding walls and fountains designed by Barry, but Landseer's lions were not placed in position until 1868.[1]

Talbot took at least five calotypes of Trafalgar Square over a period of several years and with these views he perhaps gets close to the modern concept of a news photographer by documenting current events of popular interest. The construction of Nelson's column was surrounded by a controversy which brings to mind the 'monstrous carbuncle' criticism made by a modern British Prince of the recent proposed extension to the National Gallery which itself adjoins Trafalgar Square. The flavour of the controversy is conveyed by *The Literary Gazette* of 1840:

> 'The continuance of the Nelson Column is now in abeyance; and we earnestly hope that our efforts may have had the effect of stopping altogether the consummation of this monstrous blunder. If all our arguments had failed, we should now simply appeal to the judgement of every person in London who have eyes in their head . . . let them go to the centre of the portico of the National Gallery and look upon the site, and if vexation at the committal of such an act of National shame does not prevent them, they must laugh at the grossness of the absurdity. The Pillar would stand on the right of the vista down to Whitehall, cutting off the view . . . It is impossible to conceive anything more ludicrous, and glad we were, yesterday to see that the work was not going on . . . In heaven's name, do not let the country be disgraced in this manner for a few paltry pounds, but at once determine on leaving the square to Mr. Barry's operation, and the half-dozen of labourers who are pottering about to reconcile this stubborn piece of ground, shapeless and level-less to some order or ornament and beauty. But away with these foundations for the pillar — even without it, and as yet only six or eight feet in height, they are absolute deformity.'[2]

1. See Gavin Stamp, *The Changing Metropolis*, 1984, pp.88-90.
2. *The Literary Gazette*, No. 1233 5 September 1840, p.581.

NELSON'S COLUMN AND TRAFALGAR SQUARE

83 VIEW ACROSS TRAFALGAR SQUARE TO ST. MARTIN-IN-THE-FIELDS

82 NELSON'S COLUMN UNDER CONSTRUCTION

FRANCE

Talbot made photographic trips to France in the early summer of 1843, and probably again in 1846. The 1843 visit was the more productive of the two and many fine calotypes made in Rouen, Paris and Orléans have survived to the present day. A detailed account of his movements and his interests are recorded in the correspondence.

In a letter to his mother of 15 May, Talbot writes, 'I wrote to you from Calais, and as soon as my letter was in the post I set off. You know that the stage from Calais to Haute Buisson is not exciting, but the weather was so fine that I viewed it with complacency. About Pont de Brique some very pretty shrubberies, and fertile verdant scenery . . . I slept at Montreuil. Next day, Saturday , the wind was very high and it was very cold travelling — I dined at Abbeville and then turned off the beaten Paris road, in quest of novel scenery.' By Monday Talbot was approaching Rouen: 'The first view of Rouen is very fine, from the top of a hill rather higher than Broken Hill and not more than a mile from the City — I drove to the Hotel L'Angleterre on the quai. A new suspension bridge crosses the river before my windows. Great bustle and commercial activity manifest everywhere.'[1]

Talbot photographed the suspension bridge at Rouen, almost certainly from his hotel window, and the day after his arrival, 16 May, took a number of views of the bustle and activity in the harbour. Two of the views made were sent home in a letter to Constance. Talbot's stay in Rouen was perhaps not quite as fruitful as he hoped for the fine weather mentioned earlier had changed and he evidently had an encounter with French provincial officialdom: 'I staid (*sic*) 4 days in Rouen but the bad weather continued almost all the time — I made however a pretty sketch of the Palais de Justice during an eclairci — I asked permission to draw the Cathedral but it was entirely refused . . . I suppose that it is a monopoly belonging to somebody, & I was interfering with vested rights'.[2]

Talbot left Rouen on Thursday, 18 May, for Paris, arriving on Friday evening at 9.00 p.m. By Saturday the weather had changed for the better

84 CARRIAGES BEFORE A PARIS RESIDENCE

85 THE HARBOUR AT ROUEN, 16 MAY 1843

again, 'a day of magnificent sunshine',[3] and Talbot was able to begin recording the Paris boulevards, including the view from his hotel window, which was to become Plate 2 in *The Pencil of Nature*. From Paris, Talbot went on to continue his tour via Orléans, Amboise and Avignon. The fine weather of Paris did not last for the rest of his trip but, again, this did not stop Talbot taking many interesting views.

Despite the changeable weather the French tour of 1843 must be accounted as one of the most successful of Talbot's photographic expeditions. Talbot's mother later wrote: 'Orléans & Chambord are particularly good, but I grudge the fine delicate effects of the shutters on the Parisian homes. I wish it was all [Gothic?] tracery.'[4]

1. Fox Talbot Museum, ms. LA 43-57 letter Talbot to Lady Elisabeth Feilding, 15 May 1843.
2. Fox Talbot Museum, ms. LA 43-58 letter Talbot to Lady Elisabeth Feilding, 22 May 1843.
3. Ibid.
4. Fox Talbot Museum, ms. LA 44-53 letter Lady Elisabeth Feilding to Talbot, 1 March 1844.

87 LE CHATEAU DE CHAMBORD, 1843 (VARNISHED CALOTYPE)

86 ORLÉANS CATHEDRAL, DETAIL (TAKEN WITH A LONG FOCUS LENS)

THE PENCIL OF NATURE

Between 1844 and 1846 Talbot produced *The Pencil of Nature*, the world's first book illustrated with photographs to be offered for sale to the public. It was published by Longmans and a total of twenty four calotypes were issued in six parts. The cost of the complete set of six was three guineas (£3.15). All the calotypes were made at the Reading Establishment under the direction of Talbot and Henneman. Talbot wrote a substantial historical introduction for the work and each calotype published was accompanied by a written text.

It is not clear when Talbot first conceived the idea of a substantial publication illustrated by photographs, but as early as March 1843 a correspondent was writing, 'Messrs. Longmans have informed me that it is your intention to publish Calotype views of the Cathedrals'.[1] If this was Talbot's original idea for *The Pencil of Nature*, he evidently decided to broaden the scope of his work, and in doing so demonstrated great imagination and foresight. A collection of calotypes of great architecture may, in fact, have proved more attractive to the public than the work that was finally issued. But *The Pencil of Nature* shows that Talbot, almost alone amongst the early photographers, was able to see the complete range of possibilities his new art offered in the future.

The Pencil of Nature was, on the whole, well received by critics and the public. It was recognised by *The Athenaeum* as 'the first attempt at photographic publication' and the advantages of Talbot's positive/negative process over the rival French process identified: '. . . after we have procured and well fixed a good original — any number of pictures of equal excellence and of unvarying fidelity' could be produced.[2] Of the value of the text, *The Literary Gazette* was in no doubt. Of the introduction, it writes: 'The acuteness and sagacity displayed in these trials and the philosophical conclusions drawn alike from attainment, peculiar phenomena, changes and failures, reflect great credit on Mr. Talbot's perseverance and clairvoyance.' Later it describes the calotype of the bust of Patroclus as 'really sublime in style and effect'. It goes on, 'Mr. Talbot's instructions as to the best means for taking these likenesses are of high

88 THE READING ESTABLISHMENT. TALBOT IS ADJUSTING THE LENS ON THE CAMERA.

practical value; and we have only to add another tribute of our applause to that gentleman for the skill with which he has overcome the difficulties of a first attempt at photographic publication and the excellence he has already attained in executing his designs'.[3]

1. Fox Talbot Museum, ms. LA 43-43 letter Robert Hunt to Talbot, 30 March 1843.
2. *The Athenaeum,* No. 904, 22 February 1845, p.202.
3. *The Literary Gazette,* No. 1432, 29 June 1844, p.410.

90 'LOVEJOY'S LIBRARY', READING: A POST OFFICE AND STATIONER'S SHOP WHERE TALBOT'S CALOTYPES WERE SOLD.

89 THE READING ESTABLISHMENT. HENNEMAN TIMES THE EXPOSURE AGAINST A BACKGROUND OF PRINTING FRAMES.

(THE TWO PRINTS FORM A PANORAMA)

THE PENCIL OF NATURE PLATE II

This, the second plate of *The Pencil of Nature,* was taken from a negative made in Paris in May 1843. Talbot arrived in Paris after spending four days in appalling weather in Rouen. The weather changed almost immediately as he related in a letter to his mother: 'Saturday was a day of magnificent sunshine; I never saw Paris look so well and so gay'. He went on to describe his hotel: 'It is the corner house with the Boulevards — I chose it on account of the view. My sitting room is circular.'[1]

The negative was made with a camera sited in the hotel, as the text from *The Pencil of Nature* makes clear: 'This view was taken from one of the upper windows of the Hotel de Douvres, situated at the corner of the Rue de la Paix. The spectator is looking to the North-East. The time is the afternoon. The Sun is just quitting the range of buildings adorned with columns: its facade is already in the shade, but a single shutter standing open projects far enough forward to catch a gleam of sunshine. The weather is hot and dusty.' Talbot continues in this vein and concludes: 'The instrument [the camera] chronicles whatever it sees and certainly would delineate a chimney-pot or a chimney sweeper with the same impartiality as it would the Apollo of Belvedere.'[2]

The view was described more prosaically but no less enthusiastically by a contemporary reviewer in the following terms: 'The next is an afternoon view of Paris, and takes in vast masses of building, a distant horizon of chimneys and also trees in the foreground: the effects of light and shade are remarkable, and well deserving the attention of the landscape-painter. The angles of vision too, merit his study, as determining perspective lines in a singular manner.'[3]

1. Fox Talbot Museum, ms. LA 43-58 letter Talbot to Lady Elisabeth Feilding, 22 May 1843.
2. H. Fox Talbot, *The Pencil of Nature,* notes to Plate II, 1844.
3. *The Literary Gazette,* No. 1432, 29 June 1844, p.410.

91 VIEW OF THE BOULEVARDS AT PARIS.
PLATE II, THE PENCIL OF NATURE

In the text accompanying this image, Talbot described it as an example of the 'early beginnings of a new art . . . one of the trifling efforts of its infancy, which some partial friends have been kind enough to commend.'

This is perhaps the best known example of a comparatively small proportion of Talbot's photographs where he has apparently constructed a picture to stimulate the imagination rather than simply copy or record. He described it in the following terms: 'We have sufficient authority in the Dutch school of art, for taking as subjects of representation scenes of daily and familiar occurrence. A casual gleam of sunshine, or a shadow thrown across his path, a time-withered oak, or a moss-covered stone may awaken a train of thoughts and feelings, and picturesque imaginings.'[1] Amongst all of Talbot's photographs, this is one of the most admired by modern commentators, yet there is little to suggest that his contemporaries felt it was a significant departure from his other work or worthy of particular note.

The reviewer of *The Athenaeum* damned the image with faint praise: 'It is quite as much from the opinion of the valuable suggestions which these "sun pictures" offer in the prosecution of all Art-studies, as from curiosity to witness the result of such a remarkable process, that we ever welcome Mr. Talbot's labours and recommend them to the attention of all lovers of the varied effects of light and shade'; but he followed these comments by remarking disparagingly, 'The selection of objects is sometimes not very felicitous.'[2]

1. H. Fox Talbot, *The Pencil of Nature*, notes to Plate VI.
2. *The Athenaeum*, No. 985, 12 September 1846, p.939.

92 THE OPEN DOOR. PLATE VI, THE PENCIL OF NATURE

THE PENCIL OF NATURE PLATE X

The negative of 'The Haystack' may have been taken in the autumn of 1841. In November of that year William Fox Strangways wrote to him from Frankfurt: 'Since I wrote last, I have received your beautiful Calotypes, such a packet as that I can always have through F.O. I particularly admire the Hayrick . . .'[1] Whenever it was taken, 'The Haystack' is another of the images Talbot made which shows how fascinated he was by photography's ability to show mundane objects in a new light by the meticulous reproduction of every detail, and also how the new art promised to free the conventional artist from much detailed labour: 'One advantage of the discovery of the Photographic Art will be, that it will enable us to introduce into our pictures a multitude of minute details which add to the truth and reality of the representation, but which no artist would take the trouble to copy faithfully from nature.

Contenting himself with a general effect, he would probably deem it beneath his genius to copy every accident of light and shade; nor could he do so indeed, without a disproportionate expenditure of time and trouble, which might be otherwise much better employed.'[2]

The reviewer for *The Athenaeum* took his cue from Talbot's text but his brief comments are perhaps a hint that contemporary critics were beginning to appreciate some of the problems of the new art: 'In the Haystack we have a delightful study — the fidelity with which every projecting fibre is given, and the manner in which that part of the stack which has been cut, is shown, with the latter which almost stands out from the picture, and its sharp and decided shadow, are wonderful; the foliage, however, is very indistinctly made out, and a prop placed against the stack appears as if cut in two, owing to the large amount of light which has been reflected from the object behind it.'[3]

1. Fox Talbot Museum, ms. LA 41-64 letter William Fox Strangways to Talbot, 2 November 1841.
2. H. Fox Talbot, *The Pencil of Nature,* 1844-1846, notes to Plate X.
3. *The Athenaeum,* 22 March 1845, p.202.

93 THE HAYSTACK. PLATE X, THE PENCIL OF NATURE

Talbot's remarks in his accompanying text suggest that he enjoyed taking photographs of groups and he found that 'very delightful pictures' were easily obtained. Yet, surprisingly, this is the only calotype in *The Pencil of Nature* which depicts living persons. The picture was, on the whole, well received, and the commentator in *The Athenaeum* wrote as follows: 'The figures in "The Ladder" are prettily arranged but the face of the boy is distorted, from the circumstance of its being so very near the edge of the field of the camera obscura. In looking at this photograph, we are led at once to reflect on the truth to nature observed by Rembrandt in the disposition of his lights and shadows. We have no violent contrasts; even the highest lights and the deepest shadows appear to melt into each other, and the middle tints are but the harmonising graduations. Without the aid of colour, with simple brown and white, so charming a result is produced, that looking at the picture from a little distance, we are almost led to fancy that the introduction of colour would add nothing to its charm.'[1] Yet at least one person was not enthusiastic according to a later account by Thomas Malone. Apparently the artist, Henry Collen, was present when the photograph was taken and, if Malone's report is to be believed, he felt that the view presented by the group was so clumsy that it should not have been taken at all.[2]

1. *The Athenaeum,* No. 920, 14 June 1845, pp.592-593.
2. See *The Photographic Journal,* 15 November 1860, p.33.

THE PENCIL OF NATURE
PLATE XIV

94 THE LADDER. PLATE XIV, THE PENCIL OF NATURE

THE PENCIL OF NATURE
PLATE XXIV

This is the last calotype published in *The Pencil of Nature*. Talbot made no direct comment on it in the text but the still-life image is probably another example of his expressed familiarity with the Dutch school of art. It is unlikely that the picture has any very special or symbolic significance but the inclusion of the pineapple is interesting. In the mid-19th century the pineapple was a status symbol of the upper classes. One English Lord is reported to have listed and labelled each of the immature fruits on his home-grown pineapple plants so that they could later be sent to the relatives and friends he most wanted to impress.[1] Talbot was a keen botanist and gardener and had greenhouses at Lacock where he grew and propagated rare and exotic plants. The pineapple shown is probably one of Talbot's fruits grown with his own hand and perhaps this photograph is in a small way an expression of pride in his horticultural skills.

95 A FRUIT PIECE. PLATE XXIV, THE PENCIL
    OF NATURE

1. F. H. L. Thompson, *English Landed Society in the Nineteenth Century*, 1971, p.96.

Talbot's *Sun Pictures in Scotland* was the second publication of photographs to come from the Reading Establishment. In a pre-publication notice Talbot claimed, 'Most of the views represent scenes connected with the life and writings of Sir Walter Scott'. By the 1840s the fame of Sir Walter Scott was drawing visitors to Scotland from all over the world. Talbot, evidently, was under the influence of the Scott spell and spent the autumn of 1844 in Scotland taking the calotypes which were to make up his publication.

Subscriptions were invited for the work at one guinea (£1.05) a copy. There were 98 subscribers in all, the first name on the list being the Queen.[1] But, even with royal patronage, the book was not a great success. The problem does not appear to have been any lack of interest in Sir Walter Scott or even in Talbot's process although the lack of any explanatory text may have been a contributory factor. However, the main drawback was the apparently uninspired choice of the twenty-three views by Talbot. One modern commentator has described *Sun Pictures* as, 'a dull holiday snap-shot album'.[2] This is perhaps a harsh judgement in view of the technical difficulties Talbot was forced to overcome for the views were very far from being 'snap-shots'. Yet it cannot be denied that although individual views are of interest, as a collection they lack impact. Talbot's mother, with the air of one making the best of a bad job, wrote: 'On the whole *The Pencil of Nature* is more liked than the Views in Scotland but the latter have served admirably to make the former more known'.[3]

1. V. F. Snow and D. B. Thomas, 'The Talbotype Establishment at Reading', *Photographic Journal,* February 1966.
2. Arthur T. Gill, 'More Sun Pictures', *Photographic Journal,* June 1976, p.170.
3. Fox Talbot Museum, ms. letter Lady Elisabeth Feilding to Talbot, 4 August 1845.

SUN PICTURES IN SCOTLAND

Although the Scott Monument is unfinished in this calotype, this is not the earliest known view of it (see Catalogue 120). The photograph is the second of the twenty-three views which make up *Sun Pictures*. It shows the monument just before it was completed in October 1844. Technically, this is the best photograph of the series, almost certainly because Talbot was able to use freshly sensitised paper rather than the special pre-prepared paper he was forced to use when making the more remote views.

SUN PICTURES PLATE 2

96 SIR WALTER SCOTT'S MONUMENT. PLATE 2, SUN PICTURES IN SCOTLAND

SUN PICTURES
PLATE 3

Although Talbot's *Sun Pictures in Scotland* came in for some criticism, it was in fact a considerable achievement to produce such comparatively remote views at all. Talbot explained how he overcame the technical problems of making the Abbotsford views in a letter to *The Literary Gazette* of 1852:

'I was accustomed to prepare the paper beforehand, and carry it ready prepared, in closely shut paper-holders, to the scene of action. It was in this way that in September 1844, I made a series of views of Abbotsford, the residence of Sir Walter Scott ... The paper was prepared in the inn at Galashiels, several miles distant, and it retained its sensibility during some hours sufficiently well. This can readily be effected now by several methods but at the time I speak of, eight years ago, it was more difficult of accomplishment. But this method had, in the first place, the inconvenience of being exposed to occasional failure, which required all the principal points of view to be taken in duplicate as a necessary precaution. And, secondly, it required the use of as many paper-holders as there were prepared sheets of paper; because on the supposition of the operator being unprovided with a tent, or some substitute for one, and of his not meeting with a shelter of any kind, it was a matter of difficulty to remove the photographic pictures from the paper holder and place fresh sheets of paper therein, without allowing a gleam of light to fall on them during the exchange. Add to this, that in order to have a reasonable degree of security, that the paper would keep good for twelve or twenty-four hours, it was found advisable to diminish its sensibility, so that it would not work well by an evening or failing light.'[1]

1. *The Literary Gazette,* 27 November 1852, p. 876.

97 ABBOTSFORD. PLATE 3, SUN PICTURES
    IN SCOTLAND

Sun Pictures in Scotland includes six views of Loch Katrine; three views approximately eight inches by six inches in size and three views about four inches by three inches in size. There is also a seventh view, a small scene of a Highland hut on the banks of the Loch.

Talbot's mother complained of the lack of 'clearness' of the views, due she supposed, 'to your having been in Scotland so late in the season.'[1] This lack of clearness can be rationalised as a lack of definition of parts of the print and the vague imprecise representation of the water surface which conveys an impression of an uncanny smoothness. Along with the limited range of colour and tone, to the modern eye, the image conveys an atmosphere of brooding stillness, a powerful evocation of the loneliness of the Highlands. In fact, it is likely that the mood evoked is largely a product of the technical limitations of the process, particularly the long exposures Talbot was forced to make when using pre-sensitised paper.

SUN PICTURES
PLATE 16

1. Fox Talbot Museum, ms. LA 45-111 letter, Lady Elisabeth Feilding to Talbot, 31 July 1845.

98 SCENERY OF LOCH KATRINE. PLATE 16, SUN PICTURES IN SCOTLAND

TALBOT'S ASSOCIATES

During the 1840s, Talbot was the most influential figure in British photography. Most of the pioneering photographers sought his advice, sent him specimens, or were in contact with him by one means or another. One of the consequences of this is that the large body of early photographs which makes up the Science Museum's Fox Talbot Collection includes images known, or suspected to be, by other photographers. In the past this has led to some images being wrongly attributed and it is possible that further re-assessments will have to be made in the future. Photographers whose work has been identified include, the Rev. G. W. Bridges, the Rev. Calvert Jones, Antoine Claudet, Henry Collen, Nicholaas Henneman and Nevil Story-Maskelyne. All of these people were particularly closely associated with Talbot and learned from him. The position is further complicated by the fact that Calvert Jones, Claudet and, of course, Henneman, took part in photographic sessions with Talbot. The details of these sessions are barely mentioned in the correspondence, and while speculation is interesting, which of the participants played a dominating role, technically or artistically, will probably never be known.

99 COPPER ORE VESSEL AT SWANSEA BY THE REV. CALVERT JONES

100 THE COLOSSEUM, ROME, BY THE REV. CALVERT JONES

101 FIGURE (KIT TALBOT?) CONTEMPLATING THE RUINS OF POMPEII BY THE REV. CALVERT JONES

102   GARDEN OF BENEDICTINE CONVENT,
      BY THE REV. G. BRIDGES

104   WOMAN WITH A CHILD IN HER ARMS
      (NEGATIVE) BY ANTOINE CLAUDET

103   THE BISHOP OF JERUSALEM
      (NEGATIVE), BY THE REV. G. BRIDGES

MAN IN SPANISH COSTUME

The Fox Talbot Collection at the Science Museum includes several calotypes showing a man in Spanish costume posed in a variety of stylised positions. The content of these particular images is unlike any others by Talbot and they were probably not taken by him. The lighting is strong and it is possible that the calotypes could have been made in Spain but it is perhaps more likely that they are studies produced for the guidance of a painter, possibly a part substitute for his preliminary sketches. That calotypes were made for this purpose is evident from an article in *The Literary Gazette* of 1850: 'Daguerreotyping and Talbotyping have been gradually assuming more and more importance in a fine art point of view. In portraiture, that which is properly so called, as in painting, Daguerreotyped studies have been very successfully used for getting the general effect and details of dress and other minutiae requisite for a finished picture'. The writer went on to point out that the Talbotype 'seems peculiarly adapted for assisting artists in obtaining studies of trees, weeds, stones, and ground'. More pertinently, in the light of the calotypes displayed, he goes on to review an exhibition which contained 'a very interesting collection of these studies done by an expert amateur, Mr. Elmore [not the painter] — they represent, Moors, Arabs, and Algerines, in their various costumes: and with the necessaries of dwelling places, furniture, arms, pipes and other things that convey the peculiar truth and accuracy of the picture, which could only be obtained by visiting the spot, and even then but seldom, if ever, by any of the ordinary methods of sketching.'[1]

1. *The Literary Gazette*, 28 December 1850, p.976.

ROBERT ADAMSON AND DAVID OCTAVIUS HILL

THE SCOTTISH CIRCLE
THE ADAMSON FAMILY

In this group of the Adamson family, Dr. John Adamson appears on the left and Robert Adamson is seated on the right. John Adamson was the first man to take a calotype portrait in Scotland after exhaustive and disappointing trials. His brother Robert carried the process to the finest level, producing rich, dense calotype photographs which have survived the passage of 140 years. Neither man was comfortable on the wrong side of the camera, which reflects their general diffidence in public.

107 THE ADAMSON FAMILY

It was Sir David Brewster who was responsible for Robert Adamson setting up as a photographer in Rock House, and he made it his business to promote Adamson's work thereafter. Nevertheless, Brewster had ultimately a low opinion of the calotype used for portraits: '. . . when it is employed to take portraits, particularly those of children and females, it invariably presents us with unsatisfactory results. Even if the sitter were motionless, the picture, though perfect in its outlines, would still fail to represent the delicate lines and shades of the human countenance. The defect is so great as to deter any persons from sitting for their portraits.'[1] He was also concerned by the variations in calotype portraits which undermined their claim to the truth: 'I have been very much struck with the *different* calotypes of the *same person*. In many of them, where the sitter was steady, the family likeness is scarcely preserved. Compare the enclosed one of myself with those taken by you. Does this arise from the Camera? I have seen among Mr. Adamson's Calotypes pictures of men & women in one of which the sitter was decidedly good looking and in the other hideous.'[2] 'I am still,' he added later, 'puzzled about the operation of the camera. Some cameras represent me thin, slender & not stout whereas others view me like [illegible] of the stout gentleman.'[3]

Presumably there is personal vanity as well as scientific curiosity in these remarks and Brewster felt that Hill and Adamson's portrait did him insufficient justice. John Gibson Lockhart had a different opinion. He wrote to Professor John Wilson in March 1844: '. . . that of Sir D. Brewster is by far the best specimen of the art I had ever seen. It is so good, that I should take it very kind if you would sit for the man whom Brewster patronizes *for me* . . . This is about to revolutionize book illustration entirely.'[4]

1. Review of books on photography, *North British Review,* vol. 7 1847, p.479.
2. Science Museum, ms. letter from Brewster to Talbot, 28 November 1843.
3. Science Museum, ms. letter from Brewster to Talbot, 18 April 1844.
4. Mary Gordon, *Christopher North: A memoir of John Wilson,* 1882 vol. II, p.285.

THE SCOTTISH CIRCLE
SIR DAVID BREWSTER
1781-1868

108   SIR DAVID BREWSTER

DAVID OCTAVIUS HILL
1802-1870

There are more than twenty-four individual calotype portraits of Hill in existence, which were intended mostly to serve as experimental models. The photographs show him trying out different poses and backgrounds and the effects of drapery and costume. This calotype is a more straightforward self-portrait with Hill holding a landscape in his hands as the symbol of his profession. The landscape is presumably a chalk drawing but it could as easily be either a lithograph or a calotype. The strong resemblance between the three processes made the calotype powerfully attractive to Hill as a painter.

109   DAVID OCTAVIUS HILL

THE SCOTTISH CIRCLE

GREYFRIARS' CHURCHYARD

This is the only one of Hill and Adamson's calotypes to introduce a camera into view. The two indistinct figures bent over it may possibly be Hill and Adamson themselves.

110 GREYFRIARS' CHURCHYARD,
      GENERAL VIEW LOOKING TOWARDS
      HERIOT'S HOSPITAL

JAMES NASMYTH
1808-1890

James Nasmyth, the engineer, inventor of the steam hammer and the pile-driver, was one of D. O. Hill's closest friends. Their friendship had begun in Alexander Nasmyth's house in the amicable and liberal atmosphere of interchange between painting and mechanics, and was continued in their correspondence thereafter. Nasmyth's letters to Hill are an invaluable insight into their friendship and contain enthusiastic commentaries on the calotypes. The photograph of Nasmyth led him into a situation familiar to the famous nowadays:

'I was sitting taking my tea at Birmingham Station and a gent kept looking very hard at me. At last he said is your name James Nasmyth. I says I am he and he said I thought so for I have you and your foot rule in my portmanta! his name was McClure. A fine fellow I found him and one to whom I took great liking as he told me he knows you! well and intimately. He was going up to London to establish a lithograph concern as a branch of his Glasgow and Liverpool house. I should like to meet him again and hope to do so . . . you see how faithfull your portrait is to enable me to be detected under such circumstances'.[1]

1. Royal Observatory, ms. letter from James Nasmyth to D. O. Hill, 5 August 1845.

111 JAMES NASMYTH

David Roberts was a successful landscape painter, particularly famous at this time for his series of paintings of the Holy Land. He was based in London and was of considerable help to Hill and Adamson between 1845 and 1847 in their efforts to raise interest in their calotypes in the London market.

THE SCOTTISH CIRCLE
DAVID ROBERTS
1796-1864

112 DAVID ROBERTS

Hugh Miller was a journalist and geologist who had started his career as a stonemason. He was the first to give publicity to Hill and Adamson's work in an article on 'The Calotype' in *The Witness* newspaper in July 1843. He was apparently also one of the first people to pose as a subject picture — a calotype which he described with enthusiasm in his article. This is a later, 1844 or 1845, version of the same idea, taken with the big camera. Hill placed Miller in the Disruption Picture in a strong position at the base of the central compositional triangle. His role in the Disruption itself, as the Editor of *The Witness,* the Free Church newspaper, was as important. The Rev. Dr. Thomas Guthrie said of him:

HUGH MILLER 1802-1856

> 'He was a man raised up in Divine Providence for the time and the age. His business was to fight — and like the war-horse that saith among the trumpets, Ha, Ha, and smelleth the battle afar off, fighting was Miller's delight. On the eve of what was to prove a desperate conflict, I have seen him in such a high and happy state of eagerness and excitement, that he seemed to me like some Indian brave, painted, plumed, leaping into the arena with a shout of defiance, flashing a tomahawk in his hand, and wearing at his girdle a very fringe of scalps, plucked from the heads of enemies that had fallen beneath his stroke.'[1]

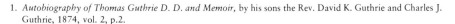

1. *Autobiography of Thomas Guthrie D. D. and Memoir,* by his sons the Rev. David K. Guthrie and Charles J. Guthrie, 1874, vol. 2, p.2.

113 HUGH MILLER

THE SCOTTISH CIRCLE

ELIZABETH RIGBY, LADY EASTLAKE 1809-1893

Lady Eastlake, like Mrs. Jameson (see Catalogue 135), was an important art critic, who was a great enthusiast for Hill and Adamson's calotypes. An enthusiastic article which appeared in the *Quarterly Review* in 1846 calls their photographs 'the beautiful and wonderful Calotype drawings — so precious in every real artist's sight, not only for their own matchless truth of Nature, but as the triumphant proof of all to be most revered as truth in art'.[1] The number of calotypes of Lady Eastlake herself are further evidence of her enthusiasm — she appears in twenty-one calotypes in the Portrait Gallery's collection, and is second only to Hill in her interest in posing as a model.

This calotype, which has been called 'A Reverie', is a subject picture rather than a straightforward portrait. The black lace and the large cross suggest a Mediterranean — Spanish or Italian — idea; the group of two naked boys suggests love. Hill has drawn a small star on the negative (presumably *not* intended as a small piece of sarcasm) which may mean a lover far away but seeing the same star. Sentimental subjects of this kind, linked to poetry, were common in painting at the time.

1. *Quarterly Review,* March 1846, p.337.

Sir David Brewster identified his own university town of St Andrews as a natural photogenic subject as early as 1840 when he wrote to Talbot: 'When you have published your method I shall immediately apply it to our beautiful ruins here which are well adapted for the purpose. We have also great & precipitous coasts which will be easily taken.'[1] The St Andrews circle, principally Brewster himself, Major Playfair and Dr. John Adamson, did not effectively master the calotype process until 1842. In the Autumn and Winter of 1842 and 1843, John Adamson taught his brother, Robert, the calotype process by using the buildings and landscape of the town as a series of testing sites for exposure times, focal range and alignment. Many of the surviving calotypes of St Andrews are repetitions of this kind which implies that they were taken before Robert Adamson set up business in Rock House, and before he met D. O. Hill. It has been argued that D. O. Hill was not involved in the St Andrews calotypes but this is unlikely.

THE ST ANDREWS CALOTYPES

1. Science Museum, ms. letter Brewster to Talbot, 23 October 1846.

115 GENERAL VIEW OF ST ANDREWS FROM
THE TOP OF ST RULE'S TOWER
A CALOTYPE PROBABLY TAKEN BY
JOHN OR ROBERT ADAMSON
WITHOUT D. O. HILL

116 ST ANDREWS HARBOUR
A CALOTYPE PRESUMABLY TAKEN BY
ROBERT ADAMSON WITH D. O. HILL

THE ST ANDREWS CALOTYPES

This particular photograph is one which can be confidently proposed as Hill's composition. The organisation is very carefully calculated, even to the satisfactory shadow of the central figure. It is an interesting comment on the whole problem of exposure times for early photography that in a case like this, the organisation time could have taken twenty minutes to an hour, with Hill running up and down stairs to judge the effect through the camera.

117 NORTH STREET, FISHERGATE

By the 1840s, the city of Edinburgh had divided into the Old and the New Town. The Old Town ran down the spine of rock between the Castle and Holyrood Palace and, from the migration of the wealthier families to the neo-classical New Town, had turned into a considerable slum crowded with distressed poor from the Highlands and Ireland. The new railways were driving into the heart of the city between the Old and the New.

THE EDINBURGH CALOTYPES

In 1845, John Knox's house was under threat, in the words of a Free Church committee formed to purchase it, because 'there was every reason to apprehend that the house was about to pass into the hands of parties whom no sound Presbyterian would wish to see in possession of it.' The committee purchased the building in 1846 and laid the foundations of a new church and school beside it. Copies of the calotypes taken by Hill and Adamson were deposited in the foundation stone of the new building.

JOHN KNOX'S HOUSE

John Knox's house stands as an example of the inherent problem of the Old Town. Important historic buildings with all the rich associations of Scotland's history were in a state of acute dereliction:

'Society, in the densely populated closes... has sunk to something indescribably vile and abject. Human beings are living in a state worse than brutes. They have gravitated to a point of wretchedness from which no effort of the pulpit, the press, or the schoolmaster can raise them. Were we to plant a clergyman in every alley, and scatter the most elevating products of literature gratuitously into every dwelling, the benefit would, I verily believe, be imperceptible. The class of whom I speak are too deeply sunk in physical distress, and far too obtuse in their moral perception, to derive advantage from any such means of melioration.'[1]

This quotation comes from a report written by William Chambers in 1840 and is one of a series of reports, including one written by Dr. George Bell, responding to the appalling typhoid and cholera epidemics which were fed by the crowded, filthy condition of the Old Town. These reports could only recommend that the Old Town be largely demolished to save the lives and health of the inhabitants. The fact that both William Chambers and George Bell were enthusiastic antiquaries who lovingly recorded the historic associations of the town, merely added to the impossible stress behind the situation.

1. William Chambers, *Report on the Sanitary State of the Residences of the Poor Classes in the Old Town of Edinburgh*, 1840, p.3.

118 JOHN KNOX'S HOUSE

THE EDINBURGH CALOTYPES

LADY GLENORCHY'S CHAPEL

Lady Glenorchy's Chapel was demolished, with other historic buildings, to make way for the building of Waverley Station.

119   LADY GLENORCHY'S CHAPEL

SIR WALTER SCOTT'S MONUMENT

The monument to Sir Walter Scott, designed by George Meikle Kemp, was reared in the neo-Classical New Town as a neo-Gothic echo of the Old. Scott's influence on the culture of Scotland and his impact in shaping the concept of the country abroad, can scarcely be over estimated.

SEE COLOUR PLATE 9
122   PRINCES STREET WITH THE
        COMPLETED MONUMENT, 1845

120   THE SCOTT MONUMENT DURING
        BUILDING, 1844

121   MASONS WORKING ON THE
        ORNAMENTAL DETAIL OF THE
        MONUMENT

William Henry Playfair's monument to Dugald Stewart is one of a group of neo-classical monuments built on Calton Hill in the early nineteenth century. It overlooks Rock House and was an obvious subject for Robert Adamson's camera. This calotype probably involves a visual pun based on the monument's resemblance to a top hat — with the tiny figure of the man in a top hat perched on the hill, which is wearing its own top hat.

THE EDINBURGH CALOTYPES

DUGALD STEWART'S MONUMENT

123 DUGALD STEWART'S MONUMENT ON CALTON HILL

THE GREYFRIARS'
CALOTYPES

Half of the calotypes taken by Hill and Adamson in Edinburgh were taken in Greyfriars' Churchyard. This can be put down to the so-called Victorian 'morbidity', an obsession with death only natural in a century when the mortality rate was abnormally high and death was commonplace. However, Greyfriars' Churchyard was one of the most picturesque sites in Edinburgh. The 17th-century tombs were particularly decorative. A number of the calotypes were also commissioned by George Harvey as studies for his allegorical painting *Children Blowing Bubbles in Greyfriars' Churchyard,* although in the event 'he had found them quite useless for the purpose for which he had wanted them'.[1]

1. *The British Journal of Photography,* 1863, p.57.

DENNISTOUN
MONUMENT

The close relationship between book engraving and carving in the 17th century makes the Dennistoun monument a natural frontispiece to the volumes of calotypes proposed by Hill to Colnaghi in 1848.

NAISMITH MONUMENT

This calotype may have been one of those taken for the painter, George Harvey. The natural symbol of the living tree, the symbol of the Christian resurrection, growing from the tomb of death was used in his painting. The reflective figure of Duncan tracing the words of the inscription derives from a classical example, used most notably by Poussin in *Et in Arcadia Ego.*

THE MACKENZIE TOMB

The subject of this calotype is distinct from the other Greyfriars' calotypes in the apparently forceful action of the figures. Sir George Mackenzie, buried in the tomb, was one of the most violent opponents of the Covenanters — the 17th-century political martyrs of the Church, with whom the Free Churchmen compared themselves. James Nasmyth was strongly, if rather oddly, moved by the photograph: 'Bloody Mackenzie's Tomb, what a perfect Romance. Oh had I the power of music what a theme I could make that suggest in the grand solemn style. There is something awfull in its character as you have calotyped it.'[1]

1. Royal Observatory, ms. letter James Nasmyth to D. O. Hill, 30 April 1843.

124 THE DENNISTOUN MONUMENT, 'THE ARTIST AND THE GRAVEDIGGER'

125 THE NAISMITH MONUMENT, WITH D. O. HILL AND THOMAS DUNCAN

126 THE MACKENZIE TOMB

PORTRAITS

The bulk of the calotypes taken at Rock House were portraits, and most of those were men. The direct strength of these portraits and the constantly inventive treatment in terms of light and pose are, like all great art, misleadingly simple and natural in appearance. There is rarely that feeling of 'quaintness' that forms a barrier between us and the run-of-the-mill old paintings, or old photographs — they look like 'real' people. James Craig Annan, who was fascinated by Hill's portraits, wrote in 1905:

'Such productions are evolved as unconsciously and as directly from nature as are the trees and flowers, and constitute a pure product; but soon there come imitators who, incompletely comprehending the work of the master, produce something resembling it in its most obvious features but lacking the subtler qualities, with the result that in course of time the pure art disappears and certain conventions and mannerisms are accepted in its place ... To present day pictorial photographers it is extremely interesting and almost humiliating to observe that on the very threshold of the photographic era there was one doing with no apparent effort what they would fain accomplish with eager strivings, and thinking so little of his achievements that when he returned to what he considered his serious work it was with a sense of having frittered away three solid years in following a most fascinating amusement.'[1]

Annan was lamenting the lost golden age of photography. The poet, Hugh MacDiarmid, used the same evidence to lament the lost golden age of Scotland:

'. . talking to two of the finest portrait photographers in Scotland who both lamented the appalling dearth of faces really worth photographing ... And they agreed with me at once when I said that it was only necessary to ruffle through the wonderful studies of Scots men and women taken by an early photographer like Dr. Octavius Hill to see how terrible the process of degeneration in the interval had been — how all the qualities of moral strength, experience of life, high intelligence, strong purpose, good judgement, individual character, force and dignity had been eliminated in the course of the past century from the faces of nearly all our people'.[2]

It requires active intelligence to realise that these portraits are 'art' and not purely 'nature', and that the impressive appearance of the sitters is a direct result of skill.

1. James Craig Annan, 'David Octavius Hill, R.S.A. 1802-1870', *Camera Work*, July 1905, p.17.
2. Quoted in Kenneth Buthlay, 'Hugh MacDiarmid: Where Extremes Meet', *MacDiarmid: An Illustrated Biography,* Christopher Wright, 1977, p.9.

PORTRAITS
SAMUEL AITKEN

The calotype of Samuel Aitken is one of those most obviously inspired by Raeburn. By choosing a low angle and a horizontal format, Hill has achieved an element of monumental solidity in a small photograph which is a successful translation of a Raeburn model.

127   SAMUEL AITKEN

SIR WILLIAM ALLAN
1782-1850

Sir William Allan was the President of the Royal Scottish Academy at the time this photograph was taken. He was sufficiently interested in the calotype process to arrange a pose for the watercolourist, John Harden, in November 1843 and probably arranged his own pose on the same occasion. The distinction between this and the calotype arranged by Hill is clear enough. Sir William made the mistake of cluttering his own picture with examples from his notable collection of armour, and the pose itself is uncomfortable. Hill's portrait is a description of the man himself.

This photograph was used by John Watson Gordon (a later President of the Royal Scottish Academy) to paint a posthumous portrait for the Royal Academy in London. Watson Gordon wrote to David Roberts in December 1857: 'I think I have been successful, almost all his friends seem much pleased with the resemblance'.[1] Since the painting was a direct transcription from the photograph, this is scarcely surprising.

1. National Library of Scotland, ms.9994 fo.45 letter from John Watson Gordon to David Roberts, 17 December 1857.

128   SIR WILLIAM ALLAN

Mrs. Isabella Begg was the youngest sister of the poet Robert Burns. She was widowed early and left to rear nine children by her own efforts running a village girls' school. She provided Robert Chambers with much information for his life of Burns. With a resurgence of interest in the poet in the 1840s, she was accorded the use of 'a picturesque cottage near the banks of the Doon, and immediately adjoining the public road leading from Ayr to the poet's monument', in response to a suggestion made by William Chambers in 1842 that 'there was a great wish to have Mrs. Begg planted somewhere about the spot of her brother's nativity'. Once planted, Mrs. Begg found herself entertaining 'Hundreds upon hundreds from every corner of the United Kingdom and from the Continent and America . . .' as a living relic of her brother.

   This portrait is an expression of Hill's own enthusiasm for the poet. It is also a powerful portrait of an individual, described in her obituary thus: 'Hers was the natural manner which art cannot communicate and which is beyond convention. Mrs. Begg was quite a lady without attempting it, just because she was every inch a woman.'[1]

1. *Isobel Burns, A memoir by her grandson,* 1891, pp.67 and 2.

PORTRAITS

ISABELLA (BURNS) BEGG 1771-1858

129 ISABELLA (BURNS) BEGG

This powerful portrait is an accurate expression of a forceful personality. Alexander Campbell was described admiringly by John Stuart Blackie, who saw him as a Highland equivalent of the noble savage:

 'Passing directly before Campbell of Monzie's door, I determined to call upon the tiger in his den, and in his den I actually found him. He received me with great frankness of old Highland hospitality, gave me a splendid dinner of venison-tripe and full-bosomed grouse, with a magnum of most excellent claret, capped with a tumbler of brandy-and-water . . . He took me through all his various and strange museums, introducing me to his magnificent deer-hounds and mingled deer-stalking and good fellowship with pious scraps of Gospel and Revival hymns in a manner quite original and refreshing. I should not have missed the acquaintance of this man for £100; he is full of natural vigour and nobleness, but like a wild horse has never been accustomed to the rein, and is not quite understood by the quiet jogging people of whom the respectability of this world is mainly made up.'[1]

1. *The Letters of John Stuart Blackie to his Wife,* ed. Archibald Stodart Walker 1910, p.169. Letter dated 18 September 1867.

ALEXANDER CAMPBELL OF MONZIE 1812-1869

130 ALEXANDER CAMPBELL OF MONZIE

PORTRAITS

JAMES DRUMMOND
1816-1877

SEE COLOUR PLATE 10
131 JAMES DRUMMOND

James Drummond was a history painter — the artist of such elaborate and detailed scenes of Scottish history as *The Porteous Mob* (National Gallery of Scotland). The sale of his effects after his death included a substantial group of photographs, including over 250 of Hill and Adamson's calotypes, and he was, in the 1850s, a member of the Photographic Society of Scotland.

The portrait of Drummond is one of the most direct of Hill and Adamson's calotypes, independent and forceful in composition and in lighting.

WILLIAM ETTY 1787-1849

Despite the technical faults of this photograph — the blank spot where the chemicals have not been absorbed on the negative and the slight blurring of the unsteady sitter — this is one of the more effective portraits taken with the big camera. William Etty came to Edinburgh for only two days on 16 and 17 October in 1844, to show his brother his three major paintings, *The Combat, Benaiah slaying two lion-like men of Moab* and *Judith*, which had been purchased by the Royal Scottish Academy. At a reception hurriedly organised for him, he apologised for his appearance: '. . . so totally unexpected was this brilliant reception that I did not put in my carpet bag a second coat, so that I am obliged to appear before you in my travelling costume.'[1] The slightly crumpled, hurried look of this photograph is thus an accurate reflection of the circumstances in which it was taken.

William Etty's reputation as a painter was very high in Edinburgh. It was all the more gratifying to Hill that he proved to be enthusiastic about the calotypes: 'Etty saw in them revivals of Rembrant, Titian and Spagnoletto.'[2]

1. *Edinburgh Evening Courant,* 2 November 1844.
2. Private collection ms.letter from D. O. Hill to David Roberts, 25 February 1845.

MISS ETTY

Miss Etty was the daughter of Captain Charles Etty whose return from his travels after thirty-one years was described by his brother in enthusiastic terms: 'He has ploughed the bosom of the ocean for many years, he has awed the pirates of the Batavian Seas; he has tracked the tiger and bearded him in his lair.'[1] She came with her uncle and father to Edinburgh and was photographed on the same occasion.

1. *Edinburgh Evening Courant,* 2 November 1844.

132 WILLIAM ETTY

133 MISS ETTY

Charlotte was D. O. Hill's daughter by his first wife, Ann Macdonald. She was too young to appear in more than one or two of the calotypes, but the pose of 'sleep' was an easy one for children.

PORTRAITS
CHARLOTTE HILL
1839-1862

134 CHARLOTTE HILL
Reproduced by courtesy of Edinburgh City Art Centre

The portrait of Mrs. Jameson has caught her tense strength of character. Samuel Carter Hall reported of her, 'although Mrs. Jameson may have been of a hard, and not a genial nature, and her temper was perhaps "incompatible", she had many rare qualities of mind, must have been a delightful companion, and was largely gifted with personal attractions.'[1] Thomas Carlyle reacted more forcibly: 'A little, hard, proud, red-haired, freckled, fierce-eyed, square-mouthed woman: it was from the first moment apparent that, without mutual loss, we might "adieu and wave our lily hands."'[2]

Mrs. Jameson was, like Lady Eastlake, an influential art critic who was impressed by Hill and Adamson's calotypes. Charles Heath Wilson in 1845 assured Hill that 'Mrs. Jameson is going to take them up strong'[3] and there can be no doubt that her critical enthusiasm would have helped greatly in launching their calotypes on the London market.

MRS. ANNA BROWNELL
JAMESON 1794-1860

1. Samuel Carter Hall, *A Book of Memories of Great Men and Women of the Age*, 1871, p.372.
2. *The collected letters of Thomas and Jane Welsh Carlyle*, vol.7 p.150.
3. Royal Scottish Academy, ms. letter from C. H. Wilson to D. O. Hill, April 1845.

135 MRS. ANNA BROWNELL JAMESON

PORTRAITS

REV. PETER JONES OR KAHKEWAQUONABY 1802-1856

136 REV. PETER JONES OR
KAHKEWAQUONABY

The Rev. Peter Jones was the son of a Welsh Methodist and a Red Indian of the Ojibway tribe. He visited Edinburgh in July 1845, and addressed a public meeting to raise money for manual labour schools 'to promote civilisation and Christianity amongst the Indians.'[1] 'What an awful and mysterious presence at a Free Church tea party'[2] said a satirical letter in the *Glasgow Constitutuonal.* John Stuart Blackie who joined him for breakfast on 11 August was not noticeably impressed: 'I have been breakfasting to-day with the illustrious Kahkenaquonaby, chief of the waving plume, from Canada. He is a tall, dark-haired, dark-eyed, rather poor looking fellow, but with a big bulging mouth.'[3]

Mr. Jones's arrival in Edinburgh was a natural opportunity for Hill and Adamson to take a picturesque photograph. The portrait of him in Indian dress is not, however, simply an opportunity seized to photograph him as a commercially saleable 'wonder' — a real live Red Indian in Edinburgh: for his individual qualities and dignity are clearly as important to the portrait as was his exotic costume. Picturesque photographs of Red Indians could have been taken six months earlier when fourteen Ioway Indians visited Edinburgh's music hall. It is likely that Hill and Adamson's reaction to this kind of public show would have been akin to Lady Eastlake's report: 'To Catlin's Exhibition. Four men Indians and three women on a table: it is a disgusting sight to see savages performing antics for display, which are only defensible in their own woods, as being done in earnest; and what fools they must think us for caring to see them.'[4]

1. *Edinburgh Evening Courant,* 29 July 1845.
2. Satirical letter from 'Anti-humbug', *Glasgow Constitutional,* 15 November 1845.
3. *The letters of John Stuart Blackie to his wife,* ed. Archibald Stodart Walker 1910, p.117.
4. *Memoirs and Correspondence of Lady Eastlake,* ed. Charles Eastlake Smith 1895, p.123.

MRS. KINLOCH OF PARK

137 MRS. KINLOCH OF PARK

Contemporary opinion regularly condemned the coarseness of the calotype process as unsuited to the delicacy required for female portraits. It is certainly true that Hill and Adamson's portraits tend towards strength rather than delicacy, and the more ladylike, ringletted women are rarely amongst their better portraits. Mrs. Kinloch is, however, an excellent example of a lighter, prettier kind of portrait, proving that the calotype, when correctly handled was capable of great delicacy of effect.

A rare attempt to show action in a calotype. It is not clear whether the pose was Hill's idea — a sketch for a sporting picture — or a result of Mr. Laing's own anxiety to be pictured as a dashing athlete.

PORTRAITS

MR. LAING

Of all Hill and Adamson's calotypes, this has the most direct, challenging intimacy. In compositional idea it relates to Sir Joshua Reynolds's portraits of women and children but lacks the sweetness of his pictures. The girl's lowered head and upward glance have far more individuality and potential aggression.

MARY McCANDLISH

SEE COLOUR PLATE 11
139 MARY McCANDLISH

John Ban Mackenzie was described as 'The handsomest Highlander of his day. Tall and of magnificent physique and "upright in appearance as in character".'[1] He was piper to the Marquis of Breadalbane, and won both a first prize and a special gold medal from the Highland Society. This portrait may, however, prove to be another John or Ian Mackenzie — Ian Dall Mackenzie who died about 1870 aged about 79. He was 'a first rate performer and blind' and was known as the 'fair-haired piper'.[2] This is presumably a portrait taken for Hill and Adamson's proposed volume on *Highland Character and Costume*.

JOHN BAN MACKENZIE 1796-1864

1. Royal Scottish Pipers Society, ms. *Notices of Scottish Highland Pipers* . . . by Lieutenant John MacLennan, revised and added to by Major I. H. Mackay Scobie.
2. I am indebted to Hugh Cheape for this information and for the reference.

Jimmy Miller was the son of the surgeon, Professor James Miller (see Catalogue 162). Hill called this photograph 'The Young Savage' and presumably intended it, like the calotype of Mackenzie, to be an illustration for the volume on *Highland Character and Costume*.

JIMMY MILLER

138 MR. LAING

140 JOHN BAN MACKENZIE

141 JIMMY MILLER

PORTRAITS

MARQUIS OF
NORTHAMPTON
1790-1851

Although the calotype is not technically a very good one, this is one of the more effective portraits taken during the British Association meeting in York in 1844. Northampton was the President of the Royal Society but Hill would have been interested in him as an influential connoisseur of art. David Roberts showed a portfolio of the calotypes at Lord Northampton's house the following Spring, urged on to it by Hill: 'I must feel highly pleased that you think them worthy of being shewn at the Graphic Society as at Lord Northampton's. His Lordship I had the honour to Calotype at York, and succeeded in making what I think a singularly Rembrantish & very fine study.'[1]

1. Private collection, ms. letter from D. O. Hill to David Roberts, 25 February 1845.

CHARLES WILLIAM
PEACH 1800-1886

Charles William Peach was officially a coastguard in Fife. He was also a naturalist and geologist and a friend of Hugh Miller. He spoke at the British Association in York in 1844 and this calotype may have been taken there rather than in Edinburgh.

MRS. ANNE RIGBY
1777-1872

Mrs. Rigby, like her daughter Elizabeth (Lady Eastlake), was a relaxed and interested sitter for the calotype. William Etty's remark that he saw in the calotypes 'revivals of Rembrant, Titian and Spagnoletto' relates to this photograph which is a small-scale domestic version of the grand full-lengths of Titian and has the personal dignity of a 17th-century Dutch portrait. A curious feeling of familiarity in this photograph is explained by its resemblance to the later painting by Whistler of his mother in a similar pose, wearing an old-fashioned white cap and painted in monochrome. As Anna Matilda McNeill, Whistler's mother was a close friend of Mrs. Rigby's daughters in the 1840s and she may well have owned a copy of this photograph.[1]

1. I am indebted to Margaret MacDonald for this information.

142 MARQUIS OF NORTHAMPTON   143 CHARLES WILLIAM PEACH   144 MRS. ANNE RIGBY

Charles Edward Stuart (*alias* Charles Stuart Hay Allan) was one of two brothers who claimed descent from Prince Charles Edward Stuart, and hence a right to the crown. They were self-elected romantic figures who lived in a tartan-hung hall and produced works on Highland dress of dubious authority. To an innocent eye they were the embodiment of melancholy grandeur — living out the Jacobite twilight. To a cynic, they were less attractive: 'The man was dressed in all the extravagance of which the Highland costume is capable — every kind of tag and rag, false orders, and tinsel ornaments which could be heaped on an ill-made clumsy person; the whole surmounted by a face very like the portraits of Charles II, but nothing like the descriptions of the Pretender.'[1]

1. *Journals and Correspondence of Lady Eastlake,* ed. Charles Eastlake Smith, 1895, p. 55.

The strength of this portrait lies both in the natural features of the sitter and in the lack of detail visible in her dress. Her shawl or cloak has been deliberately used to cover the printed dress so that the character in her face will be balanced by strong uncluttered lines between her shoulders and hands.

D. O. Hill owned a group of engravings after Watteau and followed his example in admiring the elegance of the back view. This portrait is unidentified but may prove to be Lady Mary (Baillie) Haddo.

PORTRAITS
CHARLES EDWARD STUART 1799-1880

UNKNOWN WOMAN

SEE COLOUR PLATE 12
146 UNKNOWN WOMAN

UNKNOWN WOMAN

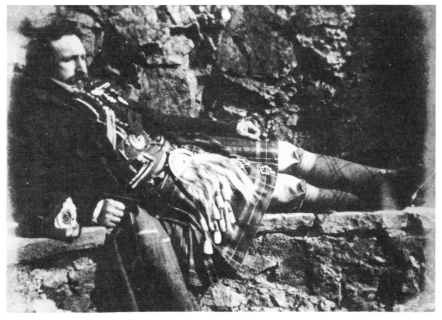

145 CHARLES EDWARD STUART

147 UNKNOWN WOMAN

GROUPS

One of the more appealing characteristics of the poses Hill devised for group calotypes was a kind of natural gothic engineering. He persuaded people to act as architecture, supporting and leaning on each other in a series of apparently comfortable shapes and compositions that result in an endearing sense of intimacy between the figures in a group. The uncomfortable reality of mechanical supports which often lay behind these groups is rarely evident in the completed effect.

GEORGE TROUP AND WILLIAM GIBSON

This is one of the most successful 'study' groups for the Disruption Picture. The two men are convincingly placed 'reading' the book and engaged in active concentrated debate. The subtle use of side lighting has enabled Hill to bring forward the face of the man behind, at the same time using the light falling on Gibson to act as a background silhouetting Troup's face — neatly balancing out the two men in terms of dark and light.

SOPHIA FINLAY AND HARRIET FARNIE

Like the sleeping portrait of Chatty Hill, this group relates to a conventional taste for pictures of children asleep — a convenient convention for painters faced with over-active children as subjects. In this instance the theme of the picture is made more convincing by the puppy flat out on the chair — adding to the question of exposure time, the additional calculation of how long it took to wear out the dog.

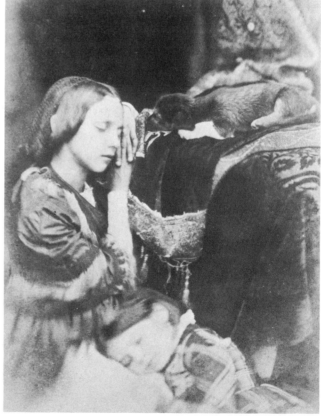

Hill and Adamson must have spent at least a day taking photographs at Merchiston Castle, experimenting with their big camera in 1844. Because of the technical difficulties experienced with this camera, most of the calotypes from the session failed. This, a large group of schoolboys, some in fancy dress, is amongst the successes.

The group of the Finlay children, Arthur, John Hope and Sophia, is one of the cleverest and most attractive of Hill's compositions. Three small children have been kept still in a tight, neat pyramid built on a flight of steps, occupying less than half the compositional space but giving a convincing idea of childhood play.

    As an extraordinary footnote to this photograph, Sophia Finlay lived to a great age, bequeathing her own album of calotypes directly to the Portrait Gallery in 1937, nearly a hundred years after this picture was taken.

GROUPS
MERCHISTON CASTLE SCHOOL

AT THE MINNOW POOL

SEE COLOUR PLATE 13
151   AT THE MINNOW POOL

150   MERCHISTON CASTLE SCHOOL

GROUPS

D. O. HILL AND
WILLIAM BORTHWICK
JOHNSTONE

This group is characteristic of the relaxed pose Hill was able to achieve with artist friends, although it is not as spontaneous as it looks. A support holding Johnstone in position can be seen between the two men.

William Borthwick Johnstone was a variable artist whose work was thought to take after different painters in turn. Appropriately enough, in view of his practical appreciation of others' work, he became the first director of the National Gallery of Scotland in 1858.

THE MISSES
DOUBIGGAN
(or MISSES HAMILTON)

Women's costume, involving a greater range of material and pattern than men's at this period, offered more opportunities (as well as more hazards) for picturesque treatment. In this picture, Hill has encountered the contemporary sentimental and economical habit of dressing sisters alike. He has reduced the overwhelming effect of gingham by giving the older girl her cape but has then exploited the idea of sisterly unity by making a circle of their arms — echoing this circular coin-shape by turning their heads into medallion profiles.

152 D. O. HILL AND WILLIAM BORTHWICK
JOHNSTONE

153 THE MISSES DOUBIGGAN (OR MISSES
HAMILTON)

The large-scale calotypes required particularly careful manipulation and support for the sitters. The apparent naturalness of this group depends on a whole scaffold of unnatural supports, as can be seen from a failed negative of the same group. The positioning of the books and hat is simultaneously a part of the composition and a method of concealing its structure.

Professor Alexander Campbell Fraser was Professor of Logic and Metaphysics and is presumably shown here as taking a class. The other figures are the Rev. James Walker, the Rev. Robert Taylor, the Rev. John Murray, the Rev. John Nelson and the Rev. Dr. William Welsh.

The sentimental analogy between young girls and caged birds — poised for flight, love and womanhood but still tender, fluttering and sweet — is used here to strengthen a composition of two tentative girls, in a convincingly endearing group. This photograph is another of the rare examples (see also Catalogue 114) of Hill drawing on a negative; in this case, he has added the bird to the cage.

GROUPS
PROFESSOR ALEXANDER CAMPBELL FRASER TEACHING

MISS ELLEN AND MISS AGNES MILNE

154 PROFESSOR ALEXANDER CAMPBELL FRASER TEACHING

155 MISS ELLEN AND MISS AGNES MILNE

FANCY DRESS AND
GENRE PHOTOGRAPHS

Several of the calotypes by Hill and Adamson show figures in fancy dress or exotic costume. They reflect a taste for genre and for the anecdotal and literary in contemporary painting. Some may relate to *tableaux* staged by Hill, while others are identifiable as 'illustrations' of scenes from the novels of Sir Walter Scott.

'THE MONKS OF
KENNAQUHAIR'

This calotype, a scene from Water Scott's novel, *The Abbot,* together with about thirty similar fancy dress photographs, makes it likely that Hill and Adamson were planning to publish a series of illustrations to Scott. The three men in the photograph were all painters and members of the Royal Scottish Academy. The calotype is a reflection of the elaborate *tableaux* which David Wilkie had made popular in the 1830s — living pictures which required elaborate preparation and lasted only as long as the people in them could remain still. The readiness of the Scottish painters to dress up and turn themselves into pictures proved invaluable to Hill when it came to organising group photographs. Their professional experience in posing at length, whilst continuing to look natural, is responsible for most of the apparently relaxed calotype groups. The seriousness of this kind of photograph can be judged by the fact the Leitch has apparently shaved off his hair for the session.

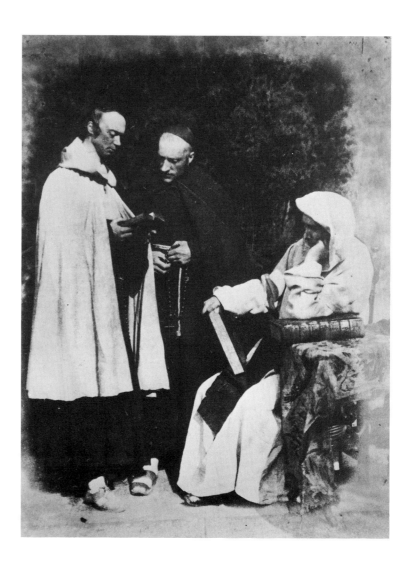

156 'THE MONKS OF KENNAQUHAIR',
WILLIAM BORTHWICK JOHNSTONE,
WILLIAM LEIGHTON LEITCH AND
DAVID SCOTT

Patrick Byrne was a blind Irish harpist. He was trained initially in a Belfast musical academy set up especially to teach the harp to the blind — an idea based on the tales of the great blind harpists of the past, aimed at recreating a golden age of music. He visited Edinburgh in 1845, and was involved in the Waverley Ball on 1 April — a fancy dress ball to raise money for the statuary on the Scott Monument. Byrne was enlisted to perform as 'The last Minstrel striking his harp to the last lay' in one of a group of *tableaux* arranged by artists (possibly including Hill).

Hill wrote to Lady Ruthven, when sending her a group of calotypes, 'The Harper, whose costume is made of a Blanket and plaid shows how simply one might get up pictures of the old world.'[1]

1. Royal Scottish Academy, ms. letter D. O. Hill to Lady Ruthven, December 1847.

FANCY DRESS AND GENRE PHOTOGRAPHS

PATRICK BYRNE
1797(?)-1883

In Sir Walter Scott's writing, he regularly stepped back from his subjects to discuss them as though they were paintings — certain of his passages were effectively worked out for painters to copy. This particular group comes from *The Antiquary*, a meeting between the Antiquary's daughter and the independent 'licensed', blue-gown beggar: 'Edie Ochiltree, old man and beggar as he was, had apparently some internal consciousness of the favourable impressions connected with his tall form, commanding features, and long white beard and hair. It used to be remarked of him that he was seldom seen but in a posture which showed these attributes to advantage. . . The young lady, as she presented her tall and elegant figure at the open window, but divided from the courtyard by a grating, with which, according to the fashion of ancient times, the lower windows of the castle were secured, gave an interest of a different kind, and might be supposed, by a romantic imagination, an imprisoned damsel communicating a tale of her durance to a palmer, in order that he might call upon the gallantry of every knight whom he should meet in his wanderings.'

Mrs. Cleghorn was Lord Cockburn's daughter, and the photograph was taken at his house, Bonaly Tower.

MRS. CLEGHORN AND JOHN HENNING

157 PATRICK BYRNE

158 MRS. CLEGHORN AND JOHN HENNING
AS MISS WARDOUR AND EDIE
OCHILTREE

FANCY DRESS AND GENRE PHOTOGRAPHS

MR. LANE AND MR. LEWIS (?)

It is not clear who the sitters are in this photograph although their costume looks authentically oriental. They reflect the current enthusiasm for travel in the Middle East which gave rise to the paintings there of David Wilkie and David Roberts. It has been suggested that these two men were Edward William Lane, who translated the *Arabian Nights,* and John Frederick Lewis, who also painted Middle Eastern subjects, but it seems more likely that they were less distinguished travellers with a taste for fancy dress.

MARY AND MARGARET McCANDLISH

This group is one of four calotypes with Margaret McCandlish posing as a milkmaid (her milk pail is on the right) which seem to be the only rustic photographs Hill organised. One of these calotypes is known as 'The Gowan' (i.e. daisy), so Hill may have had in mind Robert Burns's poem 'To a Mountain Daisy' — which is essentially a reflection on the brevity and uncertainty of life. Margaret McCandlish's pose, lying on the ground with her head propped on her hand, could be meant as the old-established pose of thoughtful melancholy.

159 MR. LANE AND MR. LEWIS (?)

160 MARY AND MARGARET McCANDLISH

This group photograph, of James Ballantyne, Dr. George Bell and D. O. Hill is an echo of the companiable sociability of Edinburgh society. James Nasmyth recalled his father's house in a letter to Hill in 1856: 'ah sirrah! them was the days for right pleasant songs, when old 47 [York Place, the Nasmyth home] was in its glory and Finnan Haddies, Ale of potency and most worshipfull toddy sent each its radiating aroma around and erected cracks worthy of being put in print . . .'[1]

1. Royal Scottish Academy, ms. letter James Nasmyth to D. O. Hill, 10 December 1856.

FANCY DRESS AND GENRE PHOTOGRAPHS

EDINBURGH ALE

161 EDINBURGH ALE

This picture is an involved literary joke. Hill, posing as hung-over, is propped against the plinth bearing a classical head turned away from the sight. The head is 'The Last of the Romans', Cassius, described by Shakespeare's Julius Caesar to Antony, thus:

> '. . . he reads much;
> He is a great observer, and he looks
> Quite through the deeds of men; he loves no plays
> As thou dost, Antony; he hears no music;
> Seldom he smiles, and smiles in such a sort
> As if he mock'd himself, and scorn'd his spirit
> That could be moved to smile at any thing'[1]

An edge is given to the joke by the fact that the Professor James Miller, taking Hill's pulse, was a temperance reformer attempting to solve the terrible problems of poverty and drunkenness in the heart of Edinburgh.

'He greatly daring, dined' is a pun on the verse inscribed on Phaeton's gravestone in Ovid's *Metamorphoses*: 'He, greatly daring, died'. There may have been a secondary pun in Hill's mind, that he like Phaeton is attempting to harness and control the sun's chariot in making his 'sun pictures'.

1. William Shakespeare, *Julius Caesar*, Act I Scene ii, lines 200-206.

THE MORNING AFTER

162 THE MORNING AFTER 'HE, GREATLY DARING DINED'

THE NEWHAVEN CALOTYPES

Newhaven was a fishing village on the Firth of Forth outside Edinburgh. The fishing community was a distinct society and the fishwives who sold the fish in Edinburgh were markedly independent and confident women, notable also for their picturesque dress. The Newhaven fishwives were hard bargainers when selling their fish and in bad weather raised the price because 'It's no fish ye're buying the day, it's men's lives'. The dangers were real enough in the small unprotected boats the men used. When Hill and Adamson advertised six volumes of calotypes in 1844, the first of the series was to be *The Fishermen and Women of the Firth of Forth*. Hill referred to the project again in April 1845 in a letter to David Roberts: 'We are preparing Fishwives for a book, and have done some fine things lately',[1] but they never published a separate volume on the subject. The Newhaven photographs are, nevertheless, famous as amongst the most powerful and beautiful of Hill and Adamson's work.

1. Private collection, ms. letter D. O. Hill to David Roberts, 26 April 1845.

JAMES LINTON

The prominence of the name on the boat's side in this calotype suggests that it was intended for use as a frontispiece to the volume of photographs on the fishermen and women.

THE NEWHAVEN
CALOTYPES

164   WILLIE LISTON 'REDDING
      [PREPARING] THE LINE'

165   'HIS FAITHER'S BREEKS' OR 'KING
      FISHER'

166   MRS. BARBARA FLUCKER OPENING
      OYSTERS

THE NEWHAVEN CALOTYPES

MRS. ELIZABETH HALL

Justifiably one of the most famous of the calotypes, this is a most satisfactory composition, exploiting the solid curve of the basket and the soft folds of the striped skirt.

167 MRS. ELIZABETH HALL

MRS. ELIZABETH HALL AND ANOTHER FISHWIFE

The bulky and distinctive dress of the fishwives, its solid folds emphasised by the stripes, gave them a sculptural dignity remarked on by Dr. John Brown who reviewed the calotypes in 1846: 'These clean, sonsy, caller, comely, substantial fishwives, — what a refreshing sight! As easy, as unconfined, as deep-bosomed and ample, as any Grecian matron. Indeed, we have often been struck, when seeing them sitting together round their oyster creels, with their likeness to those awful and majestic women, the Fates of the Elgin Marbles, the casts of which are in the Gallery of the Royal Institution [the building occupied by the Royal Scottish Academy].'[1] The shallow focal plane of the calotypes and the strongly cast shadows, emphasised the resemblance to classical bas-reliefs, especially in this kind of composition with its feeling of processional movement.

SEE COLOUR PLATE 14
168 MRS. ELIZABETH HALL AND ANOTHER
     FISHWIFE

1. Review of the Royal Scottish Academy exhibition, *The Witness,* 22 April 1846.

THE NEWHAVEN CALOTYPES

ALEXANDER RUTHERFORD, WILLIAM RAMSAY AND JOHN LISTON

169 ALEXANDER RUTHERFORD, WILLIAM RAMSAY AND JOHN LISTON

The idea of 'The Letter' was a conventional device for giving focus to a picture, which derived from 17th-century Dutch *genre* painting. It added a certain tension and doubt to the composition — Was it good news? Was it a love letter? Was it sad? At a time when so many Scots emigrated and died abroad without seeing their families and friends again, letters had an importance they have now lost, and a picture of this kind had a strong emotional appeal.

'THE LETTER'

170 'THE LETTER', MARION FINLAY, MRS. MARGARET LYALL AND MRS. GRACE RAMSAY

THE CALOTYPE USED AS A 'SKETCH' FOR PAINTING

It was the recognition of its practical use for painters — its potential as an *aide-mémoire* — that first aroused D. O. Hill's interest in photography. The photograph could serve as a substitute for the preparatory drawing or sketch. All of the calotype portraits of ministers who were subsequently depicted in Hill's painting, *The Signing of the Deed of Demission,* were conceived in this way. Other calotypes may have served a similar purpose.

THE SIGNING OF THE DEED OF DEMISSION

Hill's great painting, *The Signing of the Deed of Demission*, usually known as the Disruption Picture, was the original cause of his meeting Robert Adamson. Sir David Brewster 'got hold of the Artist — shewed him the Calotype, & the immense advantage he might derive from it in getting likenesses of all the principal characters before they dispersed to their respective homes. He was at first incredulous, but went to Mr. Adamson, and arranged with him the preliminaries for getting all the necessary Portraits'.[1] It was fortunate for photography that Brewster overbore Hill's scepticism; less fortunate for his painting, which took twenty-three years to finish. There can be little doubt that Hill's growing enthusiasm for the calotype portraits led him into painting more than 450 recognisable faces in an exercise which a friend called 'the weary Disruptive Portraiture which must have lain like an incubus on his genius'.[2] The resulting effect was described, with some justice, by a less friendly voice, as 'potatoes all in a row'.[3]

Hill originally intended to issue an engraving of the painting but in 1866 he commissioned Thomas Annan to take a photograph of it. Annan ordered a camera especially from Dallmeyer and printed the copies in three sizes in the new, permanent carbon process.

1. Science Museum, ms. letter from Sir David Brewster to W. H. Fox Talbot, 3 July 1843.
2. Samuel Carter Hall, review of the Royal Scottish Academy exhibition, *The Art Journal,* April 1868, p. 65.
3. Sam Bough, quoted in Sidney Gilpin, *Sam Bough, R.S.A.,* 1905, p. 124.

171 THE SIGNING OF THE DEED OF DEMISSION   Photograph from the painting by David Octavius Hill

Hill's original sketches for his painting show a far greater freedom of composition than the painting that finally emerged. In this sketch he has introduced a dramatic depth to the picture with a single high light-source bouncing off the table in the centre. In this and in the arched top he may be following the composition of Thomas Duncan's painting *Wishart Dispensing the Sacrament before his Execution*, which was bought by Alexander Hill at the sale of Duncan's collection on 21 June 1845. The need to present so many accurate portraits in the painting would have prevented Hill from completing it to this design.

THE CALOTYPE USED AS A 'SKETCH' FOR PAINTING

THE SIGNING OF THE DEED OF DEMISSION

172 SKETCH FOR THE SIGNING OF THE
DEED OF DEMISSION
DAVID OCTAVIUS HILL, OIL SKETCH
Reproduced by courtesy of the Free Church of
Scotland

THE CALOTYPE USED AS A 'SKETCH' FOR PAINTING

THREE PORTRAIT SKETCHES

These three sketches are practical evidence of Hill's ability as a portrait painter. It is often assumed in the histories of photography that Hill was merely a landscape painter, unable to paint portraits, and that only his conversion to photography enabled him to paint the Disruption Picture. Since Hill undertook the project before meeting Robert Adamson and had already begun sketching during the Assemblies of the Free Church, he cannot have had serious doubts of his ability to paint several hundred portraits. These sketches show that he was eminently capable and could certainly have finished the painting without the help of photography.

The portraits are unidentified and it is not possible to link them with any confidence to faces in the finished Disruption Picture. Hill is not known to have intended any other painting involving a group of ministers, so it is reasonable to assume that he painted these particular portraits for the Disruption Picture and decided not to use them.

The difference in the angle and direction of the lighting in the three paintings suggests that Hill was thinking of each man in relation to a particular position in the group and had calculated the light sources in the final painting with this in mind.

173-175 THREE PORTRAIT SKETCHES OF
MINISTERS
DAVID OCTAVIUS HILL, OIL ON
MILLBOARD
Reproduced by courtesy of Miss Aileen
Graham

These two photographs must date from May or early June 1843. They are 'sketches' for the Disruption Picture of the kind which Hill exhibited from 12 July 1843 in his brother's gallery in Princes Street to raise interest in his projected painting and to encourage subscriptions for engravings of it. They are distinguished from the later calotypes because they are purely sketches — the lack of attention Hill has paid to the background in both cases is uncharacteristic of his later work.

THE CALOTYPE USED AS A 'SKETCH' FOR PAINTING

FREE CHURCH COMMITTEE AND DUNBARTON PRESBYTERY

176   FREE CHURCH COMMITTEE

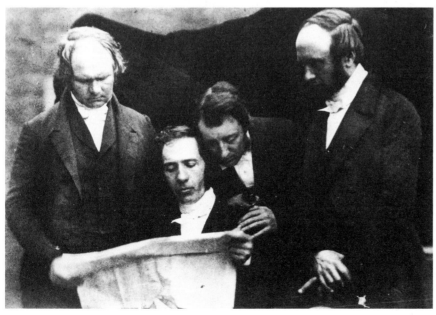

177   DUNBARTON PRESBYTERY

THE CALOTYPE USED AS A 'SKETCH' FOR PAINTING

REV. DR. ROBERT SMITH CANDLISH 1807-1873

The Rev. Dr. Robert Smith Candlish was one of the main organisers of the Disruption, described by Lord Cockburn as 'not eloquent, but a clever and effective speaker.' Hill's original plan for his Disruption painting proposed a central preaching figure, an idea which changed with Dr. Gordon's suggestion that he make the dominant theme of the picture the 'act of sacrifice'. Hill invited Dr. Gordon to be calotyped between 10 and 13 June 1843 and it may be that Gordon had this discussion with him whilst being photographed. Since this is a noticeably inept photograph, it is reasonable to suppose it is an early one, taken whilst Hill was still experimenting to see what the process was capable of.

The negative is characteristic of a failed calotype. The erratic standards of paper-making and the adulterated chemicals all too common, meant that failures of this kind were inevitable and it is a tribute to Adamson's skill that he regularly achieved success with the calotype. The composition of the photograph makes it a sketch in the true sense. Hill was clearly thinking of a pose useful to his picture, not of a composition capable of standing in its own right, which most of his later 'sketches' are (see for instance, the calotype of Dr. George Bell). By ignoring the surroundings, he has given us a clear view of the practical difficulties of portrait photography, and especially portraiture with an element of faked action. Dr. Candlish's outstretched arm is clamped at the wrist, the strut of a second support comes up diagonally behind, a man sitting on a chair stops him from swaying to and fro — and despite all this the left hand holding the book has shaken and spoilt the pose. Candlish was evidently an active if not twitchy speaker, and a chalk sketch done during the assembly (Fig. 25) exhibits a similar movement.

1. *Journal of Henry, Lord Cockburn, 1831-1854*, vol. II, p. 39.

FIG. 25   REV. DR. ROBERT SMITH CANDLISH
PREACHING
DAVID OCTAVIUS HILL, DRAWING
Reproduced by courtesy of the National
Gallery of Scotland
(DETAIL)

178   REV. DR. ROBERT SMITH CANDLISH

Dr. Macfarlane is the central figure in Hill's finished Disruption painting and symbolises the 'act of sacrifice' inherent in the Disruption. The breach within the Church of Scotland and the founding of the Free Church was impressive to many bystanders because it was an establishment revolution — middle-aged and elderly men, comfortably established with dependent families, were throwing away their own security. Lord Cockburn for one was profoundly moved: 'When this is done under no bodily persecution, with no accession of power, from no political motive, but purely from dictates of conscience, the sincerity of which is attested by the sacrifice not merely of professional station and emoluments but of all worldly interests, it is one of the rarest occurrences in moral history. I know of no parallel to it.'[1] Patrick Macfarlane was the first to sign the Deed of Demission, and as the incumbent of Greenock, which was the richest living in Scotland, was in financial terms the man who sacrificed most.

1. *Journal of Henry, Lord Cockburn, 1831-1854*, vol. II, p. 26.

THE CALOTYPE USED AS A 'SKETCH' FOR PAINTING

REV. DR. PATRICK MACFARLANE 1781-1849

The portrait of George Bell is a good example of the standard of pose Hill adopted after experiment. The use of a table, chair or books to prop arms and hands in a comfortable and apparently relaxed manner, often enabled him to dispense with the obtrusive clamps, although it can be seen that a head support has been touched out on the negative. This photograph is characteristic of the calotypes Hill used in the Disruption Picture — useful as sketches but capable of standing on their own as portraits. George Bell is represented, like Hill himself, in the painting as he was in the 1860s, an older whiskered man (see Fig. 26). Dr. George Bell was, with the Rev. Thomas Guthrie, one of the most forceful agitators for slum clearance and the amelioration of conditions in the squalid High Street of Edinburgh.

DR. GEORGE BELL DIED 1889

179   REV. DR. PATRICK MACFARLANE

180   DR. GEORGE BELL

FIG. 26   DETAIL FROM THE DISRUPTION PAINTING

THE CALOTYPE USED AS A 'SKETCH' FOR PAINTING

REV. DR. THOMAS CHALMERS AND HIS GRANDSON

The calotype group of Thomas Chalmers and his grandson, Thomas Chalmers Hanna, is one of the series of large photographs taken at Merchiston Castle in 1844. The calotype is not technically one of the best but the image was much admired by Dr. John Brown in a review of the portraits of Chalmers published in February 1848: 'Mr. Hill's calotypes we like better than all the rest; because what is in them is true, is absolutely so, and they have some delicate renderings which are all but beyond the power of any mortal artist; for though art is mighty, nature is mightier — "it is the art of God". The one of the Doctor sitting with his grandson "Tommy" is to us the best — we have the grandeur of his form — his bulk — like one of the elder gods.'[1] John Brown was a close friend of Hill and probably expressed his opinion of this calotype to him directly. In the event it was this calotype which Hill chose as the basis of his memorial portrait of Chalmers.

1. *North British Review,* February 1848.

181   REV. DR. THOMAS CHALMERS AND HIS
       GRANDSON

Hill's memorial painting of Thomas Chalmers drew on several of the Merchiston Castle calotypes for its inspiration. The picture is symbolic in intention. It is an allegory of life and death, youth and age, with the butterfly and the swallow as symbols of the brief summer lived between. The stone ball, which Hill has adopted from other photographs, may be a symbol of Chalmers's terrestrial life — the material world, overgrown with living plants but yet a soulless stone. It stands in the light patch of Chalmers's earthly life in opposition to the sundial seen through a doorway in a garden bathed in light, making the shadow on the door's threshhold an adumbration of death.

The picture is a visual elucidation of Dr. John Brown's criticism of Hill's work, made in 1846: 'He has a rich, versatile, rapid, facile mind, crowded with thick-coming fancies; but he wants concentration to turn all these to account, — to make them all work to his bidding and body themselves out . . . they have also a minuteness of observation, with a delicacy of fancy, that make everything he does bear the impress of himself, and of none else; but there is sometimes a provoking carelessness, and even feebleness in execution, and harshness of contrast. These show that his power of performance, — of sustained effort, — is not equal, or at least not by his will made equal to his conception'.[1] The painting of Chalmers is regrettably not equal to Hill's idea. He has lost the strength of Chalmers's face and made a completely unsatisfactory rendering of the boy's head.

1. Review of the Royal Scottish Academy exhibition, *The Witness*, 22 April 1846.

THE CALOTYPE USED AS A 'SKETCH' FOR PAINTING

182 REV. DR. THOMAS CHALMERS AND HIS GRANDSON
DAVID OCTAVIUS HILL, OIL PAINTING

Hill probably painted his memorial of Chalmers with the idea of engraving it. The picture subsequently belonged to his brother, Alexander, who was a publisher of fine art engravings. One of the brothers commissioned the lithographer, John Le Conte. He used both the painting and the photograph to produce the engraving and it is an interesting comment on the skill of the contemporary engraver, that he was able to correct Hill's mistakes, so that the engraving is a better translation of Hill's ideas than the painting.

183 REV. DR. THOMAS CHALMERS AND HIS GRANDSON
JOHN LE CONTE, LITHOGRAPH

THE CALOTYPE USED AS A 'SKETCH' FOR PAINTING

LIFE STUDY (DR. GEORGE BELL)

This is the only known life study by Hill and Adamson. It was presumably intended as a study for painters, although the identity of the subject may suggest a medical purpose. The very bright light falling on the shoulder probably shows Hill and Adamson using the mirror ordered from Thomas Davidson. The exaggerated effect — the bleaching out of detail on the shoulder and the equal lack of detail in the shadowed face — may well have been accidental. Since the eye will adjust to light and dark areas in a way that the camera could not, they may have found the result unsatisfactory.

ENGRAVINGS OF VELAZQUEZ'S SURRENDER OF BREDA

One of the earliest books illustrated by photography was Sir William Stirling's *Annals of the Artists of Spain*. The calotypes for this were taken by Nicholaas Henneman in Reading, and include copies from Velazquez engravings.

Hill and Adamson produced over a hundred copies of the *Surrender of Breda* using three different negatives and also photographed four other Velazquez engravings. There is no direct evidence that Sir William Stirling approached Hill and Adamson to illustrate his book, either before he went to Henneman or when Henneman was having difficulties producing the prints, but this is the simplest explanation of what is otherwise a striking coincidence. The calotypes produced by Hill and Adamson were larger than those by Henneman and it may be that they were proposing to charge too much for Sir William. It is more likely that this is a direct case of Hill and Adamson falling foul of Talbot's patent — a commercial use of the calotype which Stirling would want to market in England.

The large group of these calotypes in the Portrait Gallery's collection provides an interesting comment on the variability of the process. The colour range of the prints varies from the pale washed-out sepia commonly thought typical of the calotype to the rich reddish and purplish browns characteristic of Robert Adamson's work.

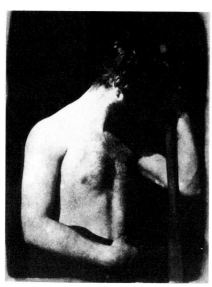

184 LIFE STUDY (DR. GEORGE BELL)

185 ENGRAVING OF VELAZQUEZ'S SURRENDER OF BREDA

Hill and Adamson probably travelled to Linlithgow on the train and several of their calotypes taken there show the railway station. Hill's friendship with the railway engineer, James Miller, involved him in producing a series of lithographs of the Glasgow and Garnkirk Railway in 1832, and in 1848 he painted the Ballochmyle Viaduct. The calotypes of Linlighgow may have been taken with a similar idea in mind. Hill's affection for this particular photograph can be seen in a drawing of the Rock House interior where it hangs in the parlour by the piano (Fig. 27).

LINLITHGOW TOWN HALL

186 LINLITHGOW TOWN HALL
Reproduced by courtesy of Edinburgh City Art Centre

FIG. 27 INTERIOR OF ROCK HOUSE

LIGHT IN PAINTING AND IN THE CALOTYPE

VIEW OF PERTH FROM THE NORTH

Hill's painting of Perth is a good example of his interest in 'aerial perspective', that is, the painting of light and distance in a landscape. Perth itself has been subordinated to the river and sky and the whole picture has been painted in terms of a particular luminous pale-grey wet light.

187 VIEW OF PERTH FROM THE NORTH
DAVID OCTAVIUS HILL, 1826
OIL ON CANVAS
Reproduced by courtesy of Perth Museum and
Art Gallery

ON THE QUAY AT LEITH

This little painting is concerned with stone buildings, canvas-rigged ships and passing figures. It is a less obviously atmospheric subject than the air and water in the view of Perth, but it is equally involved with the question of light. The picture explores the way the light filters through the sails on the left to make coloured shadows, and bounces back off the buildings on the right so that the dark areas are lightened by the reflections.

188 ON THE QUAY AT LEITH
DAVID OCTAVIUS HILL, 1826
OIL ON BOARD
Reproduced by courtesy of the National
Gallery of Scotland

LIGHT IN PAINTING AND IN THE CALOTYPE

DURHAM CATHEDRAL

189 DURHAM CATHEDRAL

YORK CATHEDRAL

Hill and Adamson carried the big camera to York in September 1844, where they succeeded in taking a number of impressive calotypes. Lady Eastlake and James Nasmyth were particularly taken with the success of these photographs. Hill, though he had reservations about the calotypes taken on this trip said that 'a few of them were among the best things I have tried'.[1] He added later: 'The big ones in so far as the figures were concerned did not turn out well — though the architecture was very wonderful'.[2]

1. Private collection, ms. letter from D. O. Hill to David Roberts, 25 February 1845.
2. Private collection, ms. letter from D. O. Hill to David Roberts, 29 December 1846.

190 YORK CATHEDRAL
Reproduced by courtesy of the Royal Museum of Scotland

LIGHT IN PAINTING AND IN THE CALOTYPE

TREE AT COLINTON

SEE COLOUR PLATE 15
191   TREE AT COLINTON

THE GROUNDS OF MERCHISTON CASTLE SCHOOL

192   THE GROUNDS OF MERCHISTON
CASTLE SCHOOL
Reproduced by courtesy of Glasgow
University Library

Details of plants and trees would in theory have been of great practical use to Hill in his landscape painting. In practice, Hill and Adamson took only two really good tree studies because of the simple problem that the photographic chemicals reacted very slowly to green. This calotype is effective because it relies on the defined shape of the branches filling the structure of the photograph like the veins of a leaf, and the foliage behind is defined only as a broken pattern of reflected light.

This is one of Hill and Adamson's most ambitious photographs using the mirror camera. The chemically-insensitive green of the trees and the grass photographed against the bright sunlight proved an almost insuperable problem for the camera, made worse by imperfections in the paper of the negative, and no contemporary print of this negative is known to exist. The photograph is composed in terms of exaggerated light effects. It is given structure by the line of the wall and the curve over the gateway, which echoes the upward curve of the tree branch following through the trees to make a visual circle of light in the centre of the composition. The open doorway and the apparent path of light with the three figures bring the line of the eye curving back into the centre foreground. The calotype was a failure but no less remarkable for that.

Bonaly Tower was the home of Lord Cockburn, judge and Solicitor-General for Scotland. Cockburn was a sociable man who greatly enjoyed gatherings of friends at Bonaly and he regarded the calotype as an extension of his sociability. One of his letters to Hill encouraged him to organise another calotype session in 1847: 'Will you be free next week? Should we not have another Calotype day — Is Allan in Town? And Harvey? [Sir William Allan and Sir George Harvey]. Any day next week will do for me. As soon as I hear from you I shall try to get some figures engaged; but the Grouse and the Queen have rather thinned the Town'.[1] The session or sessions at Bonaly, like that at Merchiston Castle, enabled Hill to direct groups and single figures within a landscape setting. This photograph of the Bonaly Lodge uses the figure of John Henning dressed as Edie Ochiltree (see Catalogue 158) as a small picturesque figure, a point of interest, in the landscape tradition.

1. Royal Scottish Academy, ms. letter Lord Cockburn to D. O. Hill, 16 August 1847.

LIGHT IN PAINTING AND IN THE CALOTYPE

THE LODGE AT BONALY

The dramatic use of angled lighting in this calotype has turned a potentially dull group into a series of satisfactory shapes of light and dark — the dark gun and carriage lighting up the centre of the picture with reflected light and the three cocky shapes of the mounted soldiers silhouetted against the sky balancing out the officers occupying the foreground.

LEITH FORT ARTILLERY

194   LEITH FORT ARTILLERY

193   THE LODGE AT BONALY

Hill took a number of photographs of the Gordon Highlanders at Edinburgh Castle in April 1846 as studies for his painting of Edinburgh from the Castle (*Edinburgh Old and New* now in the National Gallery of Scotland). This group especially, is a remarkably powerful, nearly abstract picture — a clear demonstration of the life in the very coarseness of the calotype process.

92ND GORDON HIGHLANDERS AT EDINBURGH CASTLE

SEE COLOUR PLATE 16
195   92ND GORDON HIGHLANDERS AT EDINBURGH CASTLE

LIGHT IN PAINTING
AND IN THE CALOTYPE

THE CHALMERS FAMILY

This calotype group is one of the most important taken by Hill and Adamson using his big camera. Hill and Adamson appear to have taken over Merchiston Castle School, where Thomas Chalmers's brother, Charles, was headmaster, probably for a whole day and possibly longer.

There are three versions of this group of which this is the most successful. The deliberate use of angled back-lighting which obscures rather than delineates the faces of the group, the strong pool of light in the foreground and the large stone ball reflecting the light of the sun make this a photograph of light as much as a photograph of the Chalmers family. The strong emotional and intellectual feeling which surrounded Thomas Chalmers as the leader of the Free Church make it likely that Hill would have tried to include some indication of the heroic ideal Chalmers would have suggested. It could therefore be that the stone ball at Chalmers's feet symbolises the world, and that the falling sunlight is also the light of Christianity illuminating both Chalmers and the small stone world.

It was probably this photograph which so impressed James Nasmyth that he wrote to Hill in 1845: 'Pray do not forget to try your hand at a realization of Dr. Chambers (*sic*) & Family that is of all your compositions that most noble and paintably effective. Oh do put it to canvas.'[1]

196 THE CHALMERS FAMILY

1. Royal Observatory, ms. letter from James Nasmyth to D. O. Hill, 30 April 1845.

Hill's painting is a memorial tribute to Robert Adamson and their partnership. Adamson's camera is set up on the dark slope of Calton Hill to the left and Hill's easel is in the light 'studio' garden of Rock House on the right, balancing the opposite sides of the picture as the opposites of death and life. The small figure coming through the doorway onto the path may be carrying the big camera. The composition moves down into the Calton burial ground, a 'Valley of Death' symbolic of Adamson's passing rather than his actual resting place (he was buried in St Andrews). The eye is then drawn up past the lit cross of salvation on a grave to the south where the city of Edinburgh is painted filled with misty light as a real symbol of the heavenly city and the resurrection.

This eminently touching and personal tribute to Robert Adamson was presumably painted by Hill for himself or for the Adamson family. It may be that Hill was inhibited from painting a memorial portrait of Adamson because the calotypes of him are so lacking in character or confidence, but he was following a serious precedent in painting a landscape as a memorial. He would have known both Turner's *Peace – Burial at Sea*, in memory of David Wilkie, which was exhibited in the Royal Academy in 1842, and Constable's earlier tribute to Joshua Reynolds exhibited in 1836.

IN MEMORIAM

197   IN MEMORIAM: THE CALTON
DAVID OCTAVIUS HILL
OIL ON PANEL
Reproduced by courtesy of Edinburgh City Art
Centre

BIBLIOGRAPHY

H. J. P. Arnold, *William Henry Fox Talbot, Pioneer of photography and man of Science*, 1977.

R. Brettell, R. Fluckinger, N. Keeler and S. Kilgore, *Paper and Light: The Calotype in France and Britain 1839-1870*, 1984.

David Bruce, *Sun Pictures, The Hill-Adamson calotypes*, 1973.

Gail Buckland, *Fox Talbot and the Invention of Photography*, 1980.

Colin Ford and Roy Strong, *An Early Victorian Album. The photographic masterpieces (1843-1847) of David Octavius Hill and Robert Adamson*, 1976.

John Miller Gray and others, *Calotypes by D. O. Hill and R. Adamson . . . Selected from his collection by Andrew Elliot*, 1928.

Ian Jeffrey, *A Concise History of Photography*, 1981.

Katherine Michaelson, *A Centenary Exhibition of the Work of David Octavius Hill 1802-1870 and Robert Adamson 1821-1848*, 1970.

Alison Morrison-Low and J. R. R. Christie ed., *'Martyr of Science' Sir David Brewster 1781-1868*, 1981.

Sara Stevenson, *David Octavius Hill and Robert Adamson. Catalogue of their calotypes taken between 1843 and 1847 in the collection of the Scottish National Portrait Gallery*, 1981.

D. B. Thomas, *The First Negatives*, 1964.

Mike Weaver, *The Photographic Art. Pictorial Traditions in Britain and America*, 1986.

The Real Thing. An Anthology of British Photographs 1840-1950, Arts Council of Great Britain exhibition, 1975.

From Today Painting is Dead. The beginnings of photography, Arts Council of Great Britain exhibition, 1972.

Printed in Scotland for Her Majesty's Stationery Office by Holmes McDougall Limited, Edinburgh. 762218/4623 C40 7/86